Build the Damn Thing

Build the Damn Thing

How to Start a Successful Business If You're Not a Rich White Guy

KATHRYN FINNEY

PORTFOLIO | PENGUIN

Portfolio / Penguin
An imprint of Penguin Random House LLC
1745 Broadway, New York, NY 10019
penguinrandomhouse.com

Copyright © 2022 by Kathryn Finney

Penguin Random House values and supports copyright. Copyright fuels creativity, encourages diverse voices, promotes free speech, and creates a vibrant culture. Thank you for buying an authorized edition of this book and for complying with copyright laws by not reproducing, scanning, or distributing any part of it in any form without permission. You are supporting writers and allowing Penguin Random House to continue to publish books for every reader. Please note that no part of this book may be used or reproduced in any manner for the purpose of training artificial intelligence technologies or systems.

PORTFOLIO and PORTFOLIO with javelin thrower design are registered trademarks of Penguin Random House LLC.

Book design by Cassandra Garruzzo Mueller

ISBN 9780593329269 (hardcover)
ISBN 9780593329276 (ebook)
ISBN 9798217182442 (paperback)

The authorized representative in the EU for product safety and compliance is Penguin Random House Ireland, Morrison Chambers, 32 Nassau Street, Dublin D02 YH68, Ireland, https://eu-contact.penguin.ie.

154026569

For Christian—
I can't wait to see the world you build.

CONTENTS

FOREWORD
xi

PROLOGUE: A BUILDER'S STORY
xv

INTRODUCTION

Getting Started: How to Build the Damn Thing

1

STEP 1

Get Your Mind Right: How to Build Your Internal Foundation

17

STEP 2

Your Personal Success Toolbox: How to Gather the Tools to Build Your Company

51

STEP 3

You're NOT Your Customer: How to Make Sure Your Business Solves a Problem

67

STEP 4

Product-Market Fit: How to Turn Your Solution into a Money-Making Business

83

STEP 5

Squad Goals: How to Build an Amazing Team

123

STEP 6

Getting the Bag: How to Get the $$$ You Need to Grow Your Company

167

EPILOGUE

Breathe. You Just Built the Damn Thing.

225

ACKNOWLEDGMENTS

227

NOTES

229

INDEX

237

The Universe Is Conspiring for Your Greatness

FOREWORD

Guy Kawasaki

Build the Damn Thing is a book for the rest of us. That is, people who didn't win the pattern-recognition lottery that perpetuates the old ways of entrepreneurship. In geek terms, this book provides a core dump of the theories and practices that are necessary for more people, especially more people of color, to build great businesses.

The times are changing. Entrepreneurs are not all rich white men from Stanford. I assume that you're not one of them, and if you are, you'll learn just how hard it is to build a business as a person of color.

I first met Kathryn in 2009, when I organized and moderated a keynote panel at SXSW featuring successful women in tech. I've followed her storied career ever since—from selling her media company to building the paradigm-shifting organization digitalundivided to her newest bold endeavor, the venture studio and its fund, Genius Guild. Fast-forward more than ten years later: I interviewed her again for my podcast because, as I said, Kathryn is the startup whisperer for diverse entrepreneurs.

Kathryn represents the kind of leadership, courage, and ovaries that the future demands. She's an investor and entrepreneur who's kicking ass and denting the universe. She doesn't give a shit about playing by the

FOREWORD

rules of the current elite and status quo. And this is what it takes to build great companies, organizations, and institutions that break barriers in this post-pandemic, post-science, post-truth world.

Every great startup begins with the belief that there must be a better way, but if you want to build fast, then you need the type of practical and tactical knowledge that Kathryn has infused in this book.

So what are you waiting for? BUILD THE DAMN THING.

I just took a DNA test, turns out I'm 100 percent that bitch.

Lizzo, patron saint of boss bitches

PROLOGUE

A Builder's Story

How many times have you opened a business book and read some piece of advice that was true ... except for you?

The year 2009 was very, *very* good for me. Six years earlier, I had turned my love of discount shopping into one of the first lifestyle blogs, called *The Budget Fashionista* (*TBF*). The site had grown into a seven-figure media empire. Along the way I'd become an online influencer before Instagram and TikTok even existed. My first book had been picked up by a major publisher and became a hit, I had a monthly spot on NBC's *The Today Show*, and my blog was landing six-figure endorsement deals from major companies like T.J. Maxx and Tide. I was even living in a deluxe apartment in the sky in New York City.

Life was good ...

That is, until I decided to join an incubator program in New York.

As a Black woman building her second tech-enabled business before the word "startup" had an entry in Urban Dictionary, joining an incubator was *supposed* to offer me the ability to connect with other startup founders, to be in a space where entrepreneurship was celebrated, and to get mentorship from people who have built successful companies. An incubator was *supposed* to have curriculums that walk entrepreneurs through the phases of building a company and connect founders with experienced mentors.

I had a killer idea. I wanted to leverage the 1.1 million weekly unique visitors to my blog empire to create and market a beauty subscription brand for Black women. But I knew from building TBF that building a company is lonely work, especially when you're first getting started and your idea is a dream. You can *see* your idea, you can *feel* the idea, but you might not know the steps to turning your idea into a business.

There I was, a Yale-educated scientist running one of the most popular lifestyle sites in the blogosphere. I thought that with those credentials the startup world would welcome me with open arms.

I was wrong.

I didn't know it quite yet, but the startup world wasn't created for someone like me. In fact, it wasn't created for the 233-million-plus Americans—and the billions of people in the world—who aren't white men. This was especially true for the early 2000s New York startup community. At the time, New York was like the plus-one to Silicon Valley's robust, tech-bro-centered culture. In the early days of the startup world, a successful city was one that had a local company that was sold for more than $1 billion, aka a unicorn company, because those were the types of companies that made venture capitalists rich. It wasn't until 2013 that New York would have its first unicorn company, Tumblr.*

As soon as I entered the incubator-from-hell, I was met with the harsh reality of pattern matching. Pattern matching is why it's easier for some groups (tech bros, aka white guys from Stanford) to get the funding and support they need to grow their companies than it is for others (everyone else).

---

*Tumblr, home of cat memes and not-safe-for-work content, was founded in 2007 by David Karp and was sold in 2013 to Yahoo (remember them?).

PROLOGUE

The theory behind pattern matching is this: since many of the "successful founders" in the startup space have been white guys from Stanford, MIT, and Harvard, it's assumed that *all* future successful founders will likely be white guys from Stanford, MIT, and Harvard too. As Paul Graham, founder of powerhouse incubator Y Combinator, says, "I can be tricked by anyone who looks like Mark Zuckerberg."

Founders whose identity falls outside of the pattern are often seen as a "risky" investment because we're "unknown." Never mind that the obvious, but often overlooked, fallacy of pattern matching means the majority of *failed* founders have also been white guys from Stanford, MIT, and Harvard.

The idea that an American, who just happens to be Black, would be seen by another American as "unknown" or "risky" runs counter to the meritocratic and "accepting" veneer of the startup industry. If you scratch the very thin surface of this veneer, you'll find the world of startups is super lazy when it comes to dealing with actual humans. The majority of the investors deciding who receives opportunities have graduated from elite institutions and have a very sheltered worldview. I should know, as I spent several years as the "quirky Black girl" at exceptionally bougie schools like Phillips Academy Andover and Yale. Instead of putting on their Patagonia fleece vests and challenging themselves to expand their networks, they stay put and operate in this closed system. As a result they tend to give the opportunities to people like themselves. They can't see people who are different, because everyone, and everything, around them is the same.

However . . . the good part of being "100 percent that bitch" is that I didn't give a damn about what the startup world thought. I was going to build my company with or without their support. One day, feeling particularly bold after shooting a really good national TV segment on budget Halloween costumes, I volunteered to give my elevator pitch at

PROLOGUE

the incubator's weekly investor pitch session.* As I walked to the front of the large grey conference room where we had our weekly sessions, seventy people stared at me, including CEOs of tech companies and the guy who was one of the founders of the mixed martial arts league Ultimate Fighting Championship (UFC). I glanced at my husband, the only other person of color in the room, and he gave a smirk back that said, "Show them exactly who you are."

I took a deep breath, remembering that I know how to talk; I had just spoken to 30 million television viewers on my *Today Show* segment. So I put on my Minnesota smile and gave my pitch for a beauty subscription company targeting Black women. I outlined the size of the market, explained my stack,† and discussed how I would market my products to my community of over 1 million. I explained that while Black women are about 6 percent of the U.S. population, we purchase close to 50 percent of all the hair care products in this country—a market worth $2.5 billion. And that's just for shampoo and style aids. When you include styling tools like flat irons, weaves, hair accessories, etc., the market grows to an estimated half a trillion dollars.

I brought this group of mostly white dudes into the wonderful world of ethnic hair care, the world of weaves and sister locks and edge gel. And I got it done with ten seconds to spare in my three minutes of allotted time. #Winning!

Silence . . .

Silence, which didn't make sense, especially in this group of super

---

*An elevator pitch is a short explanation of your company and business in less than thirty seconds (think of it as how you would explain what you're doing if you had only the time it took to go between floors on an elevator).

†A stack is the tools (usually tech related) you are using to build your business. An example stack for, say, an e-commerce company could be Shopify (store management tool), WordPress (web content management tool), and Google Workspace (for management of communications).

overachievers who never passed up a chance to demonstrate their intelligence. The first person to break the silence was a guest mentor, Scott Heiferman, then the CEO and founder of the community site Meetup.com. He straightened in his seat and said, "That was one of the best elevator pitches I've ever heard." The other guest mentors chimed in with their praise and a few questions about the idea and next steps. I was told that I received the best feedback out of anyone in the group.

Being an overachieving Black woman, I knew I was the best, mostly because when you're a smart Black woman and you find yourself in a room where you are the only one who fits that description, you have no choice but to be the best. It's a burden that every smart Black person, smart Indigenous person, smart Latinx* person, smart Asian person, and every smart woman carries with them from the first time they unveil their full brilliance to a group of people prepared to dismiss them instantly. You learn, quickly, how to calibrate your reactions to idiocy in an effort to protect your humanity.† You quickly do a few mental calculations, thinking, "Is today the day I totally pop the eff off? Or do I put my humanity in my 'sunken place' because popping off would mean that I, and consequently other Black people, would never be allowed into the room again?"

Here's what happened next. The cohort leader, a progressive white dude named Craig who desperately needed to make sure I knew he was here to "help me" before he, too, dismissed me, turned to get feedback from the audience as a whole. Another famous tech god told me my business model was excellent but he "doesn't do Black women." To this day, I have no idea what that means. The brother of the head of the incubator,

---

*I use the term "Latinx" throughout the book in order to be more inclusive and gender neutral.
†This strategy is called "covering" and is often used by diverse entrepreneurs to downplay a negative stereotype (e.g., "angry Black woman," "spicy Latina," "passive Asian male"). It's exhausting.

PROLOGUE

the most earnest of the earnest white tech dudes, told me that he didn't think I could "relate to other Black women" because I had an accountant. One person asked me if I actually knew any fashion bloggers and another questioned whether women online were a "real" customer base.

The "feedback" continued, with one tech bro after another making narrow-minded excuses as to why I wouldn't succeed. And I found myself—like many of us who have been marginalized—feeling angry. I *hate* being angry. I'm by nature a goofy, fun-loving midwesterner.

When was the last time you met an angry Minnesotan?

I was angry that I was being asked dumb questions by people who had a hard time reconciling who they *thought* I was (somehow inferior) with who I actually *am* ("100 percent that bitch"). Angry at the fact that I wasn't able to show my full brilliance because of the intellectual limitations of others. Angry that the very industry that prided itself on being able to "see around corners" couldn't see how their own biases limited the success of 75 percent of the world. These are the same people who defy the laws of physics by landing a rocket upright, but they can't see women online as customers? They lead companies that make billions of dollars off memes created by Black people (Hello, Twitter. Looking at you, Instagram. Side-eying you, TikTok) but can't see how Black women can build businesses?

Hmm, *okay*.

This pattern-matching BS was affecting my ability to secure the bag,* so I scheduled a time to chat with the founder of the incubator, the Voldemort of Venture Capital (VVC), during his office hours. His "office" was really a small room in the middle of the larger office space of a failing startup. As I sat in the Herman Miller Aeron chair (the required chair of failed startups) in front of his gigantic glass desk, I could tell he was ner-

---

*Aka make money.

vous about being with me alone. Was it because I was Black, a woman, or both? I didn't care. At that point I already had thirty years of training in handling the fragility of privileged white dudes developed from growing up on the mean streets of Minneapolis, Minnesota. I knew the tone I had to use to make him comfortable (friendly but confident). I knew to smile as I talked, otherwise my passion for my business would be interpreted as "angry."

I relaunched into a pitch for my company. I knew he was going to love it, because what's not to love about a recession-proof market worth over a billion dollars? What investor wouldn't get geeked up about a founder with an established platform that she 100 percent owns with a monthly gig on the top-rated national television morning show, and who is married to a software engineer (free coding!)? Voldemort's eyes lit up as I explained my stack, waxing poetic about the wonders of JavaScript and Ruby on Rails. He rushed to the whiteboard* as I went deep into my business model, helping me to plot out other ways to scale the idea. Before we wrapped up the conversation, he fired off five warm introductions to investors he knew who were interested in the consumer packaged goods space. I left the meeting saying, "Fuck patterns! I got this!"

Yeah, *right*.

Here's what *really* happened. After my pitch, VVC sat back in his chair that cost more than my rent and said, "Great idea, and obviously you can do this." Then he leaned forward and said, "However, I'm going to be honest. I don't know of any investor who's invested in a Black woman. I'm not saying that you won't get investment, it's just highly unlikely that you will." Then he got up and walked to the door, signaling

---

*Startup offices often have some sort of way for you to write on a wall to do what is called "whiteboarding," aka brainstorming ideas on the wall. It's the tech-geek version of graffiti tagging.

that my time was up, saying, "Keep me posted," which is like saying, "Don't call me; I'll call you" in startup speak.

Luckily for me, I was born with the "IDGAF"* gene and a natural tendency to ignore those who attempt to limit me, a tendency fostered by parents who never once told me what I shouldn't or couldn't do. I was eventually forced out of the incubator for reasons that remain unclear to me to this day. I didn't pursue the idea of revolutionizing the Black beauty industry. Not because of my experiences in the incubator, but because The Budget Fashionista—which I 100 percent owned—was growing by leaps and bounds. So I continued to build *my own* damn thing, The Budget Fashionista, and eventually sold it in 2012 for a substantial sum.†

I went on to build *several* damn things. The Budget Fashionista, one of the first women-led blogging empires, which led to one of the first book deals by a blogger and one of the first national television appearances by a blogger. And then there was digitalundivided, a groundbreaking social enterprise that forced the exclusive world of venture capital to have a "come to Jesus" moment regarding its institutionalized racism and sexism. And now, Genius Guild, a visionary venture studio where I boldly invest in brilliant Black-led startups, including, in a full circle moment, a digital health startup named Health in Her Hue, led by a Black woman public health professional. So, VVC . . . you and your whiteboard can go and suck bricks.

We dreamers build companies because we want a creative life that we control. Entrepreneurship is the tool that helps us achieve this goal.

---

*"I don't give a fuck." Entitleds swear A LOT and so I'm claiming this right for the rest of us.
†Know that you are all you need to be successful. There's a great story that my dear friend JB shared about the singer Jessica Simpson, who in the middle of a brutal divorce from fellow singer Nick Lachey gave in to a larger settlement, telling her father not to worry because "I'm going to earn it back." Which she did . . . and then some. Simpson's net worth in 2020 was an estimated $200 million. You got this.

PROLOGUE

That is the reason why we deal with those who discount us (like I did with the incubator that didn't incubate), so that we get to our end goal (selling my company and spending a summer traveling around the South Pacific).

For Builders like me, the ability to create a life we control is worth the risk of possible failure. The possibility of creating a legacy is so great that we choose to leave the gravitational pull of a traditional career and become entrepreneurs. Imagine creating something you truly believe in, watching it succeed beyond your wildest dreams, and then getting paid for the value you've created. That's the promise of building your own damn thing.

So get the West Wing ready and let's go build.*

You GOT this.

---

*Aka getting prepared to win. According to Urban Dictionary, Kanye West said, "Get the West Wing ready" when a poll (allegedly) showed that he had 17 percent of the Pennsylvania votes in the 2020 U.S. presidential election. We all know how that turned out (TL;DR he did NOT win).

Build the
Damn Thing

> Wherever you're standing right now, you're just taking a short break.
>
> — BTS, the thousand-plus-member K-pop superstar group

INTRODUCTION

Getting Started: How to Build the Damn Thing

Think of entrepreneurship like a video game where everyone starts out on a different level. The goal is always the same: to grow your company quickly and create a life that you control. And on the surface, the rules of the game seem perfectly fair. But not everyone has the same chance of winning, because we all begin the game from very different places. Some gamers get to start out on the easy levels and are given thicker armor, special weapons, and unlimited ammo. I call these people the Entitleds. Others are forced to start on an advanced level with no armor, no special weapons, and no extra lives. I call them the Builders.

In the business world, the Entitleds are rich white guys. They start off on the easiest level possible, and they're even given cheat codes just in case they get stuck. Yeah, there are some obstacles present at this level, but they're relatively small and much easier to overcome. Even when a white male entrepreneur messes up (and they mess up often), the game keeps giving them extra lives and letting them try again from where they left off.

A Builder is anyone other than a wealthy, white, straight, cisgender male. We Builders, by default, start off at a harder level than the Entitleds.

And the more diverse identities someone has, the harder their starting level is going to be as each additional identity requires more mastery of the game to win. So if you're a white woman who is straight and relatively well-off, you might be playing on the medium level: you don't get as many lives as the Entitleds, but you still start with upgraded armor and unlimited ammo. If you're a poor Black woman, you're playing on a more advanced level, where you have to build your own weapons from whatever you can find. If you're a poor, Latinx, transgender woman, you're forced to play the game on an expert level. You have only one life and no armor. Plus, there are more monsters to kill and they move twice as fast. Beating the game is much harder for Builders.

This game is advertised as a meritocracy, a system that rewards you based only on your skills, when in fact, it's based on everything *but* merit. Builders always play on a harder level than Entitleds. Sometimes Builders play on the medium level, other times it's on the super-hard level. But the game always starts on a harder level.

ALWAYS.

There's no logical reason why Entitled gamers receive this advantage—there's nothing about Entitleds that makes them special other than the fact that they were, well, born entitled. But since they've created the rules of the game, they get all the advantages.

Most Entitleds don't even realize they have an advantage; they're too busy playing the game at their level to give much thought to people who are stuck on other levels. Many convince themselves that Builders simply aren't talented enough to make it to their level in the startup world. This quote from Michael Moritz, chairman of Sequoia Capital and one of Silicon Valley's leading venture capitalists, clearly illustrates this point.*

---

*Investopedia defines a venture capitalist as an investor who provides capital to companies exhibiting high-growth potential in exchange for an equity stake. This could be funding

We look very hard.... What we're not prepared to do is to lower our standards.... If there are fabulously bright, driven women who are really interested in technology, very hungry to succeed, and can meet our performance standards, we'd hire them all day and night.

In reality, Builders are every bit as motivated and skilled as Entitleds, but they're playing the game on a harder level. Every now and then, against all odds, a Builder is actually able to win. These stories are thrown around by Entitleds as evidence that the game is fair.

But just because this is how the game has historically been played (and won) by the Entitleds, does that mean it has to remain so?

Hell no.

You Can Build It

Keeping it 100,* many books about how to succeed in business are written by Entitled white men who have no idea of the challenges everyone else faces. Rarely do the examples of business greatness highlighted in these books feature women leaders, and none of the thirty-plus books I've read on entrepreneurship contained an example of a successful startup led by a Black or Latinx founder. The tech world promotes the concept of "out-of-the-box thinking" but can't think of any successful entrepreneurs whose very existence is out of the box.

This book teaches everything you need to know to go from idea to your first product to raising your first million dollars in investment.

---

startup ventures or supporting small companies that wish to expand but do not have access to equities markets.
*"Honest," as defined by Urban Dictionary.

You're holding a step-by-step how-to manual for us Builders looking to turn our ideas into successful startups. We, like our Entitled friends, want to lead a creative life that we control. The world of high-growth entrepreneurship, aka the startup world, is just the method in which we accomplish this goal. This book helps you translate the out-of-the-box thinking you've done your entire life into a viable, high-growth company. We cover everything from how to turn small setbacks, like finding out that your "big" idea isn't such a big idea, into pivots, and how to quickly test your idea for less than a hundred dollars using my Ugly Baby test. We also cover how to raise money for your company, through methods like crowdfunding, and how to win over venture capitalists, like myself.

I've learned a lot during my twenty years in the startup space. A LOT. I learned that if I was 100 percent authentic, even billionaire white dudes would want to invest in me. I learned the importance of timing when I sold my first company, The Budget Fashionista. I learned the power of community when leading my social enterprise. One thing that's stood out is that every successful startup goes through a few steps. Each chapter of this book walks you through these steps, one by one. Want to figure out if your brilliant idea can be an actual business? Head to Step 3 (You're NOT Your Customer: How to Make Sure Your Business Solves a Problem). Trying to figure out how to hire your first employee? Head to Step 5 (Squad Goals: How to Build an Amazing Team). Wondering what the hell is a cap table? Head to Step 6 (Getting the Bag: How to Get the $$$ You Need to Grow Your Company). Though you can read it from front to back in order, I wrote this book to be a perennial reference that you can dip in and out of when you need it. Think of it as the mentor who is always available to help you build your business.

These steps are extremely important because the old adage that "you have to be twice as good as rich, white, Entitled dudes" is especially true in the startup world. Entitleds can often skip a step (or even three or four). For Builders, anticipate that you will be questioned at every step of the process. The penalty for not knowing the answer is getting locked out of the game.

Throughout the book you will also see "Tool" sections. These are exercises that help you develop the tools you need in order to build your startup. Some tools are action oriented ("Find Your Exit Number") and some might be more thought-provoking ("Face Your Fear"). All of these elements are an incredibly important part of your startup toolbox.

You will also notice that I've highlighted a number of "Builder Traps." These are roadblocks and challenges that can limit your ability to successfully build your company. Beware and try to avoid them at all costs.

The startup world is changing . . . albeit *slowly*. In the meantime, you'll need to know a few cheat codes to get through the game. Like what do you do when a potential investor responds to your amazing pitch for a company that uses blockchain technology to manage refinanced mortgage loans with the question "What was it like growing up in inner-city Chicago?" (First, take a deep breath, and then use a version of this suggested response: "Great question, Connor! Let's set up time at our next meeting to discuss this. Now let's get back to how we're going to scale our revenue ten times in less than three months." Your goal is *always* to get to the next meeting.) Or how to respond when an investor tells you he's always been into "Asian chicks" (always have a friend/colleague/family member call you five to fifteen minutes into a meeting, so you have a way out).

So What Exactly Is a Startup?

The question seems fairly simple. Many would say a startup is any company using tech to rapidly scale its business model. Some might say it's any company that takes a systematic approach to finding a repeatable business model. Others would say those looking for capital—namely venture capital, which we will discuss in Step 6—to fuel rapid growth, and others might say a company looking to grow revenues to the point that it doesn't need any capital to fuel growth.

They are all right. A startup is simply a company interested in growing as quickly as possible in order to achieve a "positive event" for those who invested time and/or capital (money) in the company. A positive event, from the view of an outside investor, could be being bought by another company (Instagram being purchased by Facebook) or having an initial public offering (IPO) and raising money on a public stock exchange (which Facebook later did, to great fanfare). A positive event could also be the company generating enough revenue to purchase back ownership of the company from a group of investors (like Sean "Puff Daddy/P. Diddy/Brother Love/insert most recent name" Combs did when he bought out investors in his company Bad Boy).

Startups are technically small businesses. According to the U.S. Small Business Administration (SBA), any company with fewer than five hundred employees (in some industries, fewer than fifteen hundred) is considered a small business. In addition, the SBA considers a company to be a small business if it earns less than amounts ranging by industry between $750,000 and $38.5 million per year. Most startups have significantly fewer than five hundred employees, and many don't have any revenue (aka "pre-revenue"). However, there are some factors that set a startup apart from a typical small business.

The Difference Between Small Businesses and Startups

	SMALL BUSINESS	STARTUP
Scale	Locally focused	Globally focused
Business document	Business plan	Pitch deck
Use of technology	To support the business	Core to the business
Sources of funding	Loans Personal funds/bootstrapping* Crowdfunding Friends and family	Personal funds/bootstrapping Crowdfunding, venture/angel investment Friends and family
Fixed costs	High	Very low
Speed of build	Slower	Faster
Goal	Legacy	Exit

The biggest difference between a startup and traditional small business is the scale and the use of technology. Startups are looking to rapidly grow to millions of customers whereas small businesses may be just looking to serve a particular, smaller community. Startups also use technology to reach customers and run efficiently and are focused on

---

*Bootstrapping essentially means you use your own resources (your personal bank account, 401[k], etc.) to fund your business versus seeking outside support such as loans or investment.

achieving one of the aforementioned positive events. But that doesn't mean your company has to build an app to be considered a startup.

Any idea can be a startup. It doesn't have to be a "tech" product because, well, everything is now tech. When you're playing solitaire on your phone, you're doing tech. When you go through those self-service lines at your local grocery store, you're doing tech. When you start your car, hail a cab, or ride the subway (all run by computerized systems), you're doing tech. When you try to explain to your mom that she doesn't need to use full, grammatically correct sentences in her Facebook posts, you're doing tech.

Everything Is Tech. Everything Is a Startup.

The choice between building a startup and building a small business is up to you as the founder and really comes down to how big you want your company to be and whether or not you plan on using technology to help it scale. If you are looking to run a single taco truck in your neighborhood, then you're a small business; if you are looking to build a fleet of taco trucks that can be scaled indefinitely using a proprietary operating system, then you're a startup.

Startups also differ from small businesses in terms of the speed in which they develop their solution. Startups focus on moving extremely fast, meaning they make mistakes often and repair those mistakes quickly. Successful startups rarely focus on perfection, choosing instead to focus on searching for "product-market fit," which simply means making sure the product you're building has a large number of customers BEFORE you spend tons of time and money developing it. Product-market fit is one of the most important factors in the development of your company, which is why we'll go over it in great detail later in Step 4: Product-Market Fit: How to Turn Your Solution into a Money-Making Business.

INTRODUCTION: GETTING STARTED

Small businesses are the lifeblood of the American (and global) economy, and sometimes there's a tendency to look down on them in the tech space. But the categories of startup versus small business aren't static. You can start out as a small business and later decide to grow your company to be a startup, like I did with my first company, TBF Group (aka The Budget Fashionista).

Anything can be a startup, and anyone can build one. This game isn't just for Entitleds anymore. I've discovered the cheat codes, and I'm sharing them with Builders everywhere.

Why YOU Should Build Your Startup

Entrepreneurship is one of the most established ways to create wealth. Technology-enabled entrepreneurship, because of its low fixed costs (think: no office space and equipment), is one of the cheapest ways to reach scale as an entrepreneur. This is a crucial factor for Builders as members of marginalized communities, because we don't have access to the historical wealth that our Entitled counterparts do. Technology has made it easier to own your own business and, since it has reduced the actual cost of running it, to keep more of the profit.

How I Went from Epidemiologist to Media Mogul

Which is exactly what I did in 2003, when I was a newlywed living in Philadelphia, the smallest big city in the country. My father had just died. The only friend I had within a hundred-mile radius was the salesman at the Nordstrom shoe department at the King of Prussia (KOP) mall. I had over $90,000 in student loan debt from my Yale degree in epidemiology, but you couldn't pull me away from the mall. My husband suggested I write down my fashion advice as a hobby rather than spending my time (read: money) shopping.

This was before the era of fast fashion, and it was hard to find cheap clothes that actually looked good.* It was a time when the worst thing you could say to a person was that they shopped at Kmart or Target. Shopping on a budget was a sport for *middle-aged* women, not anyone young or hip. But I didn't have a choice because I was broke. Enter *The Budget Fashionista*.

I started *The Budget Fashionista* using one of the early open-source blogging platforms. Selfies hadn't been invented yet. In those days, the only way to get a photo to show up on your site was to take a picture using a standard camera, print the photo out, scan it, upload it directly to your server, and hand-code it into your web page. I had to learn HTML and how to build SQL databases to get the pair of Kate Spade sandals I bought at Nordstrom Rack for thirteen dollars to show up online.

The Growth of Blogs Since 2003

2003 (when I started *The Budget Fashionista*)	About 2 million active blogs
2006 (when my first book was published by Random House)	35 million blogs

---

*Isaac Mizrahi's line at Target, which created the modern bridge between high design and mass retail, launched six months AFTER I started *The Budget Fashionista*.

INTRODUCTION: GETTING STARTED

2012 (when I founded digitalundivided)	about 180 million blogs
2015 (when my son was born)	260 million accounts on the Tumblr platform alone
2020 (when I founded Genius Guild)	1 billion Instagram accounts

Initially, the blog was just a way for me to share all of the expertise I gained from spending so much time and money hanging out at the mall. My first post was the answer to a question from my sister-in-law, who had recently given birth to my nephew, about the best place to find a baby bag. Even though I had no children at the time, my frequent excursions to the KOP meant I knew designers had started to make high-end baby bags for new moms, a welcome relief from the massive utility bags of the past.

The Budget Fashionista *in August 2003**

---

*Believe it or not, in 2003 this was considered awesome web design.

11

I would like to say that from the day I wrote that first post I already had a grand vision of becoming the "Oprah of the internet," but actually the big vision didn't come until later. This was right after the first big tech crash, and no one had quite figured out how to make money online yet. Thanks to a new open-source blogging program called Grey Matter,* I was one of the first people outside of MIT and Stanford who could build online companies without having an advanced computer science degree. That first site was written in a language called Perl, which means it was hosted on our own servers and everything had to be hand-coded and then linked to our database. "What you see is what you get" (WYSIWYG) interfaces like Expression Engine, Blogger, and WordPress didn't exist yet.

At the time, people in geek communities had been using the web to record their thoughts for a while, but building a website was a new concept for us civilians. Since there were no online content guides to follow, I just wrote as if I was talking to my sister-in-law (in fact, sometimes I really was talking to her). Need to know how to score an invite to next weekend's Michael Kors sample sale? I could get you the hookup. Want tips on shopping for makeup at the local drugstore? I got you.

As the blog grew, it went from a side gig to a full-time small business. I even took courses at the world-renowned Fashion Institute of Technology, alma mater of big designers like Calvin Klein and Donna Karan, to learn more about the theory of fashion and how clothes are made. This led to a brief stint as a personal stylist to a number of high-powered executive women in New York.

I continued to develop and grow *TBF* until it reached over 1 million unique visitors per day and provided content to top sites like *Real*

---

*Matt Mullenweg, CEO of Automattic and one of the founders of the blogging platform WordPress, once told me how the Grey Matter platform influenced the creation of WordPress.

Simple, *Lucky* magazine, and *Cosmopolitan*. This high growth in users turned my small business into a full-fledged startup.

I became the FIRST lifestyle blogger to turn my blog into a book and the first blogger to be on a major network morning show. I did all of this while being a big Black woman with funny glasses and a sick sneaker game. I later sold that company and became one of a handful of Black women to *create and sell* a tech-enabled business.

What the Entitled Tech Bros Don't Want You to Know

Here's what the Entitleds don't want us Builders to know: Anyone can build a startup.

Period. End of discussion.

After I joined a startup incubator program I realized the tech bros in the group were intimidated by my ability to execute an idea with nothing more than my own willpower and brilliance. I'm not saying they're bad people. I'm saying their unconscious biases prevented them from seeing new opportunities. Years later, I'm one of the most successful people to come out of that program. Yet, at the time, nobody wanted to take a chance on me and my idea.

Entitleds don't want us to know that anyone can do it because then there would be more competition for them in the race. The irony is that the very technology they've built to disrupt industries from hydrogen fusion to hair weaves reduced or even eliminated several of the advantages only Entitleds had in the race.

For example, the use of race- and gender-based barriers to funding are rendered virtually irrelevant because it costs less than twenty dollars per month to build an online site using a WYSIWYG tool like Squarespace. You don't even need a computer, as most development can be done on your cell phone. You don't even have to know how to code to build your tech company.

Crowdfunding platforms have democratized early-stage investment, giving Builders the ability to use their networks for nondilutive funding.* The ability to leverage networks for investment and funding has been used by Entitleds for centuries to build their companies. Concepts like leveraged debt, access to enormous loans, and unlimited credit to purchase things like companies and securities, rather than monies from their personal bank accounts, are all examples of nontraditional methods used by Entitleds to build their companies.

Builders have powerful resources that we don't even recognize. For instance, my tech-savvy husband helped me code the site when I first started building *TBF*. Finding potential customers to interview for customer discovery is one of the hardest phases for new entrepreneurs, yet many of us go to churches that have thousands of members. Our families might not be able to give us seed investment, yet those family members can provide childcare or a place to live. This can save us thousands of dollars per year, which can be reinvested into our businesses.

---

*"Nondilutive" means that by accepting this funding you don't lose any ownership in your business.

Builder Trap: Different Rules, Different Resources

While we Builders have the talent, ideas, and drive, we don't have the same access to ready capital. This often means we must turn to crowdfunding or retirement savings to fund our companies.* Furthermore, our networks look different. We may have gone to UTEP instead of UTA.† Our companies may be located in Oakland instead of San Jose, in Newark instead of Manhattan, or Manchester rather than London.

This is why I'm NOT okay with the exclusion of the ideas of Builders like you and me. I'm NOT okay with blogs, tweets, and business books spreading the gospel of the world of startups while hiding the fact that the rules are different for people like us. Builders, the global majority, build companies. We build startups.

You got this.

---

*Please, DO NOT use your 401(k) to fund your business. The fees and penalties for withdrawal alone are a big enough reason.
†University of Texas at El Paso and University of Texas at Arlington.

> What you have inside is what you portray to the outside world.
>
> — Walter Mercado, world-renowned spiritual guru and (embellished) caped superhero

STEP 1

Get Your Mind Right: How to Build Your Internal Foundation

As a Builder, you are the head of your company. If you're not good, then the company will not be good either. It doesn't matter that you've invented a way to make your cat's litter box smell like cinnamon donuts or that you have so much money that your bank has its own bank. Taking time to mentally prepare yourself for the daunting task of building a company will give you a much bigger return on your investment than just jumping in.

Those of us who are moms have a saying: "If mommy ain't good, then no one is good." Moms are often the people who keep the wheels turning in a family, serving as the comforter and moral center.* If the hub—the center of the wheel—is broken, it's impossible for the spokes to turn and propel the family forward. As a mom, your self-care is also your family's self-care.

---

*This isn't to diminish the extremely important role of dads and other parental figures.

The same is also true as the CEO of your company. Your self-care is also your company's self-care. You are the hub of your company.

You bring your full life experiences to everything you do, especially building a company. You can't build anything—a company, a family, or even a fence—if you're not in a good place internally. And if you're not in a good place internally, there is no shame in stopping now.

Not everyone can or should be an entrepreneur. You could even say that choosing to be an entrepreneur is an exercise in bad judgment. Most new companies fail. Entrepreneurship is an extremely lonely endeavor, and it involves a great deal of risk, both personal and financial. Not everyone can or should assume this level of risk.

And that is okay.

But if you do want to embark on the quest for a creative life you control through entrepreneurship, preparation is key. Taking time to get yourself in a good place is the single most important thing you can do to ensure the success of your company before you build it.

Building Your Internal Foundation

There's a tendency to define success as something outside ourselves. We say, "If I just get this job/investment/partner, then I will be successful." While these types of achievements can help you along the path to success, they are external. The path to success is internal. As a Builder, there will be times when the only person who can see your vision will be you. You are your own boss, and any boss worth their weight in stock options understands that self-awareness—knowing who you are and acknowledging your strengths and weaknesses—is an extremely important part of being a great leader.

In order to build your company, you will need to get comfortable with uncertainty, risk, and failure. You must be able to manage the stress and challenges that come from the realities of building a startup. Of the hundreds of companies I've encountered throughout the years, the ones that succeeded were the ones whose founders built a strong internal foundation before executing their ideas.

Smart, successful entrepreneurs have no problem spending time on their mental and spiritual health. My dear friend Kendra Bracken-Ferguson, co-founder of the health company rē•spin with Oscar winner Halle Berry, has a formal yoga practice that she does every day. I'm a member of a group of exceptional women entrepreneurs and leaders called TheLi.st. During the COVID-19 pandemic, the CEO of the group gave its members a free month of a meditation app.[*] Getting your mind right is crucial to getting your company right.

Builder Trap: Fear of Failure

I've missed more than nine thousand shots in my career. I've lost almost three hundred games. Twenty-six times I've been trusted to take the game-winning shot and missed. I've failed over and over and over again in my life. And that is why I succeed.

MICHAEL JORDAN

---

[*]Los Angeles County also gave its residents a free subscription to the app during the height of the COVID pandemic.

As you set out to build your company, know that failure is part of the journey. Failing isn't fun, and most people quit when things don't immediately start working out.

But not you...

It can be even harder when you're a Builder because **some people expect you to fail**. There's a big difference between having *permission* to fail and the expectation that you *will* fail. *Permission* means that failure is part of the journey, not the end result. *Expectation* assumes that the journey, no matter what you do, will end in failure. It assumes the path you take is rigged and so full of sinkholes, land mines, and bear traps that no matter how carefully you walk it, you'll lose your way.

However...

I know from personal experience that you can turn the expectation of failure on its head to become wildly successful. I watched my father do exactly that. The key is to give yourself permission to have a big vision of who you want to become and not let expectations (whether internal or external) influence your ability to make that vision a reality.

The Power of Fearlessness: Defying Expectations

Long before the TV show *Happy Days,* serial killers, and dudes with bedazzled pianos,* Milwaukee, Wisconsin, was a beer factory town of

---

*The patron saint of bedazzle, Liberace, and horrible serial killer Jeffrey Dahmer are both from Milwaukee.

proud, hardworking German, Polish, and African American citizens living in the shadow of its bigger sister to the south, Chicago.

It's in this environment that my grandmother Anna Mae gave birth to my father, Robert "Bob" Finney. While my grandmother's family wasn't impoverished—they owned a house in 1940, a pretty amazing feat for people of any race—my grandmother was very rebellious and became pregnant with my father at age sixteen. Consequently, my father was raised by her parents, my great-grandparents, Walter and Lucille. In fact, he didn't know my grandmother was his mom until he was in his early teens.

Now imagine having your life turned upside down at a time when you have hormones raging through your body. The people you thought were your parents aren't really your parents. The person you thought was your sister is really your mom. This culture of silence to protect "respectability" was prevalent throughout American society in both Black and white communities, and more common than most of us would think.*

However, my dad was a young Black man in mid-twentieth-century America who wasn't given permission to mourn and struggle with life-changing information. There was no child psychologist available in his blue-collar, working-class community. A straight-A student at a racially mixed high school, he wanted to be a surgeon. When he told his white high school guidance counselor, the counselor instead explained to a young Bob Finney that his goal was beyond his reach. He should focus on learning a trade and working in the brewery.

My dad, like most young Black men in 1960s America, was *expected* to fail.

So my dad, too, started to rebel. He stole a car and found himself on the wrong side of the law. The judge who decided his fate gave him a

---

*The actor Jack Nicholson, who is of the same generation as my father, also went through a similar situation.

choice: go to jail or go to war. This was in 1964, right in the escalation of the Vietnam War. My father, who had only ever been as far as Chicago, enlisted in the army at sixteen years old. Imagine being a teenager leaving everything and everyone you've known to travel to literally the other side of the world. Imagine the fear of the unknown, of war, of the very real possibility of never coming back home.

After serving two tours in Vietnam he returned to Milwaukee and did what every good Milwaukeean did: went to work at one of the city's many breweries (in his case, Schlitz). Working at the brewery was a great job—you could make $50,000 a year in the 1970s without a high school diploma. However, spurred on by my well-educated mom, my dad went back to school while working the third shift.* He got his GED,† graduating with a 3.9 GPA, and then an associate's degree, all while supporting two children and working a full-time job.

In this time of Zoom work and Microsoft Teams, where meeting your coworkers in person feels rare, it can be hard to understand that working at a factory or brewery was more than a job, it was a community. My parents socialized with their coworkers after work. My brother and I were in Little League and Girl Scouts with their children. Schlitz would often have these elaborate Christmas parties in one of the shipping hangars, with a Santa, gifts, and lots of food.

So you can imagine the devastation when the brewery shut down.

The shutdown was quick; the brewery was open on a Tuesday and gone on Wednesday. It devastated Milwaukee. It devastated my family.

After the brewery closed down, my dad took whatever jobs he could

---

*Factories operate 24/7, so often the workday is divided into shifts. The first shift (the day shift) is usually morning to early evening. The second shift (the evening shift) is early evening to late night. The third shift, aka the graveyard shift, the shift my dad worked, started late at night and ran until early morning.
†The General Educational Development test (GED) is the standard test in the United States to demonstrate that a person has high-school-level skills.

to support the family, including driving a Little Debbie Snack Cake truck. He eventually found his way to a place called the Opportunities Industrialization Center (OIC), a network of workforce development centers founded in 1964 to train (and retrain) workers in impoverished communities. The OIC was located a few blocks away from the now-closed brewery. At the OIC, my dad took a Saturday basic C++* class taught by a computer programmer from IBM named Monroe Shaw.

I give you all this backstory because it's super important to understand the path my father had to walk in order to go from a displaced brewery worker with an associate's degree from Milwaukee Area Technical College and a job driving a food-service truck in 1983 to a senior engineer at Microsoft in 1993.

In 1980s America, there was nothing to indicate that a displaced Black factory worker with a GED could be anything more than a displaced Black factory worker with a GED. There was no Google to read about others who had turned failure into success and no Instagram to scroll through quotes from successful people displayed on floral backgrounds. There were no Jay-Zs or Nipsey Hussles, who went from gangs to superrich businessmen. There were no Oprahs or Rihannas, who rose from abusive childhoods to become billionaires.

No. There was absolutely, positively NO indication that my dad would become a millionaire by age fifty.

Except for one thing.

My father took a risk. He took a shot with the military, with his GED. He also took a shot when he met an ambitious young woman (my mom) who was definitely out of his league (and a big thanks for that for obvious reasons).

What is equally notable was that my mom gave my father, at great risk

---

*C++ was one of the early general programming languages.

to herself, permission to take shots. She gave him permission to fail. In December 1982, the month that Schlitz shut down, the Wisconsin unemployment rate was 11.5 percent. My mother saw that the possibility of a career in a growing industry and better schools for her children far outweighed the alternative of staying where she loved, near people who loved her, but in a city that was dying.

In the '80s, the average Joe (or Bob) had no idea of the possibilities of computing. The internet wasn't a thing, having a computer in your home was *super* new, and there were definitely no personal cell phones. I'm 99 percent sure my dad had other things he would have preferred to do with his Saturdays (like sleep), but he took a shot at the OIC class.

The class turned into an unpaid internship at IBM. The internship led to a job offer as an entry-level programmer at Digital Equipment Corporation (DEC), the Boston-based early pioneer in computing, in Minneapolis, Minnesota.

Geographically, Minneapolis isn't that far from Milwaukee, just a five-hour drive (three hundred miles) up I-94. But culturally, it was the other side of the moon. It was different in little ways, like how everyone's last name ended with "son" (Olson, Anderson, Nelson . . .). And in big ways: it was colder, richer, and whiter. We had a strong support system in Milwaukee; both of my grandmothers lived there, along with a large extended family. To move away from everything we knew to another city was the biggest shot my father had ever taken in his life.

The expectation was not only that my dad would fail, but by default my entire family would fail. "Friends" told my mom that putting her career on hold was "stupid" and that my father would leave her. Some told my parents that their kids would come back "white."[*]

---

[*]The terms "acting white" or "talking white" were often used within the Black community to describe those who are perceived to have success without staying rooted in the Black community. The thought was that if you obtain a level of education or success that has traditionally

STEP 1: GET YOUR MIND RIGHT

Yet for my parents, the opportunity to create a stable, creative life that they controlled was more powerful than any naysayers. So my parents, my brother, and I packed up the Chevy Cavalier and headed to the home of Prince and lutefisk,* Minneapolis.

My dad rose through the ranks at DEC and was recruited as a senior software engineer at Microsoft. He was an executive at EMC, an early data storage company, when he passed away in 2002.

The universe was conspiring for my father's greatness.

Failure Is Part of the Journey

My father's story is not unique. The path to success isn't a straight line. All successful people have stories of deep challenges. Everyone who has ever succeeded has failed, had to pivot, or taken a huge risk—sometimes all three at the same time.

As Builders, we don't get to own our success because when we fail, it doesn't just impact us, it impacts entire communities. It impacts the family members who gave us money they really didn't have to lose because they so believed in our vision. Those who put their hopes and dreams on our success become tied to our failure as well. The pressure to succeed without ever experiencing a single setback is real. But it isn't *realistic*.

For so long the ability to take risks—and building a company is *risky*—was something that only Entitleds could do. If you know that the median net worth of a Black family is $24,000, close to one eighth of that of a white family, then you are uniquely aware of the economic impact of

---

been reached only by white people, you will somehow not be able to relate to other Black people. This is, of course, the legacy of internalized racism.

*A dried fish that has been brined in lye. Yep, lye.

your mom taking a second mortgage to fund your business. If you watched your parents work at backbreaking jobs that didn't match their skill levels, just so you would have an opportunity for success, you want to show them that the sacrifice was worth it. If you're the *friend and family* whom everyone turns to for economic support, you know the impact of rededicating your resources away from them to build an idea.

Failure isn't an option when you're a Builder. Except that every successful person has failed. The trick is knowing how to fail before you hit rock bottom. The old saying that "the definition of insanity is repeating the same mistake over and over again and expecting different results" is especially true when building a company. It's hard to correct your course if you have no idea you're heading in the wrong direction. Failure shows you that you are on the wrong course and it's time for a change. Learning what doesn't work is as important as learning what does work, and that means becoming comfortable with failure and learning to overcome it.

Even Beyoncé, Queen of Winning, Has Failed

Before Beyoncé was the queen of all things fabulous, she was the head of a girl group with the most girl group of names, "Girls Tyme." The six members practiced for hours in young Queen B's parents' basement and performed in talent shows throughout Houston, Texas. The group caught a big break when they scored a spot on the popular talent show *Star Search* in 1993, by "hip-hop-rappin'" (*Star Search* host Ed McMahon's words, not mine) wearing very 1990s outfits of coordinated quilted jackets in purple, neon green, and white. The group, which included future singing star Kelly Rowland, lost *big tyme* to a rock group named Skeleton Crew.

In the aftermath of that crushing defeat, Girls Tyme broke up. Three of the other members, Ashley, Nina, and Nicky, left because their parents didn't want them wasting any more time on a group that was clearly a lost cause. As if that wasn't bad enough, Girls Tyme's manager and creative consultant called it quits too. With everyone else giving up hope and facing a lot of "No, no, no"s, Beyoncé had a tough choice to make at age *eleven*. Do I give up a dream of becoming a pop star and just be a "normal" kid? Or do I continue to give up all my free time to become a star?*

Beyoncé, being, well, *Beyoncé*, decided to stick it out. She had spent most of her childhood, close to ten years, pursuing her dream. She had gained valuable experience on how to perform on a big stage, experience she, Kelly, LaTavia, and new member, LaToya, incorporated into their new group.

She found a new manager (her dad, Mathew Knowles) and renamed the group. First they were Something Fresh, then the Dolls, and then Cliché. Finally, they settled on the name Destiny's Child. They wrote songs, practiced, and pursued talent scouts. When they finally got their chance, six years later, to perform in front of executives at Columbia Records, they crushed it, scoring the group's first record deal.

Their first Billboard top-ten single was an ode to all the rejection they faced, titled "No, No, No."

There's a difference between failing because you tried and failing because you didn't try. Builders who maintain a growth mindset know that you must try, even if success is far away. When you fail you learn valuable lessons that put you a step closer to your goal. Every time Michael Jordan missed a free throw, he studied what went wrong and corrected it. When Oprah was fired from her first anchor job at WJZ-TV in Baltimore for being "unfit for TV," she headed to Chicago and became one of the most powerful women in media. When the most decorated gymnast in history, Simone Biles, fell off the beam at her first international

---

*Check out Queen Bey's video for "***Flawless" to see how she continues to turn her experience with failure into wins. The very beginning of the video includes the first moments of their *Star Search* performance.

tournament in 2013, she practiced until the beam became one of her signature skills.

Sometimes we let the fear take over, leading to missed opportunities. The next story illustrates how this limits our potential greatness.

How Fear of Failure Killed the Best Idea for Vegas (Next to the All-Night Buffet)

I'm going to share a secret... I'm an undercover Trekkie, a fan of the TV series *Star Trek*. Nichelle Nichols's groundbreaking turn as communications officer Nyota Uhura in the original *Star Trek* series continues to influence me and generations of women scientists.* I had (have?) a HUGE crush on the actor Sir Patrick Stewart, fostered by years watching him as Captain Jean-Luc Picard on *Star Trek: The Next Generation*. I even received a scholarship from him and Amnesty International while I was a student at Yale.†

So you can imagine how annoyed I was when I read a story on the site *Collider* about how a Hollywood executive was so paralyzed by the fear of failure that he killed what would have been the most awesome project in the history of Las Vegas (and perhaps even the world): a full-scale *Star Trek* USS *Enterprise* ship in downtown.

The project was to be built in the area that is now known as the Fremont Street Experience. The ship would have been about the same lengths as the Eiffel Tower and the HMS *Queen Mary*. Inside would be a restaurant, rides, tours, and more. Just imagine having a glass of Romulan Ale at the Shipyard Bar.

---

*Both Sally Ride, the first American woman astronaut, and Mae Jemison, the first Black woman in space, credit Nichols as a major influence on their becoming scientists.
†The way Sir Patrick would say my name in his Shakespearian-trained British accent still makes my spine shiver.

STEP 1: GET YOUR MIND RIGHT

It was going to be awesome.

The idea was impressive. Projections estimated that it would rival Disney World in attracting visitors and money. The Goddard Group, the firm behind the idea, accomplished the truly herculean task of getting buy-in from ALL the parties involved in the project, including the city government, the downtown economic council, even Paramount, which owned the rights to the *Star Trek* brand. Local hotels and casinos, seeing the amount of traffic the attraction would generate, agreed to provide funding to support the building. Anyone who has ever dealt with a public or private partnership understands that getting all these folks to agree on something this big was miraculous.

After several months of organizing, selling, and getting everyone on the same page, the pitch came down to a single meeting with the then-CEO of Paramount Studios, Stanley Jaffe.

Jaffe was a seasoned Hollywood producer and insider who had become an executive at Paramount in the early 1970s. He went on to produce a string of major late-'70s and '80s hits like *Kramer vs. Kramer* and *Fatal Attraction*. He returned to Paramount as CEO in 1991, not long before the final pitch meeting for the Vegas attraction.

The Goddard Group had managed to get all the players into one room at Paramount Studios in Los Angeles. They included everyone from the mayor of Las Vegas, who flew in on a private plane with members of the downtown redevelopment project, to executives from Paramount, including the president of Paramount Studios, Sherry Lansing. Everyone was there to get the final okay from Jaffe.

So Goddard launched into their pitch with thrilling graphics and models. The excitement in the room was palpable. Everyone was impressed by the bold vision and concept. My future adult self was planning my first pilgrimage to the mothership.

Except the fear of failure took over. Jaffe was afraid of possible public humiliation.* According to Goddard, he pushed back, saying, "In the movie business, when we produce a big movie and it's a flop—we take some bad press for a few weeks or a few months, but then it goes away. The next movie comes out and everyone forgets. But THIS—this is different. If this doesn't work—if this is not a success—it's there, forever." (As it happened, Gary Goddard, the founder of the Goddard Group, later experienced his own public humiliation.)

If the project didn't work, the worst-case scenario was that they would be left with a really big, ugly structure in the middle of Las Vegas (which, frankly, wouldn't have stood out). Most baffling: the project wasn't going to cost the studio any money. All the funding had already been pledged by other Las Vegas businesses and investors. There was very little that could go wrong, and little risk for Jaffe. Maybe Mr. Jaffe would have lost his job (which he did anyway soon after this decision) and bruised his ego, but he's an Entitled, so he would have been okay.

Imagine what would have happened if he had looked past the fear of failure and okayed the project. Imagine the number of tourists who would have made a pilgrimage to the USS *Enterprise* to groove to the "Awasoruk Jam." Think about the economic impact it might have had on the community of Las Vegas. Consider the impact the merchandising might have had on Paramount's bottom line. Or even just the coolness factor of being able to visit an almost life-size replica of the *Enterprise*. A project that would have revitalized an entire city ended because of one person's fear of failure.

---

*But not too afraid, as he later produced *I Dreamed of Africa* (Rotten Tomatoes score: 10 percent).

> **Tool: Face Your Fear**
>
> Imagine what cool things you could build if you let go of your own fear of failure. The following exercise will help you do just that.
>
> One of the ways to help remove the fear of failure is to write down the worst things that could happen if your idea doesn't work out. Expressing your worst fears on paper somehow takes the bite out.
>
> So get a piece of paper. List all the worst things that could happen if your business was to fail. List all of them, even the ones that might be painful to think about. For example, when starting The Budget Fashionista, I was afraid of leaving the comfort of my very stable job as an epidemiologist. When I started digitalundivided, I was afraid of losing the money I made from selling The Budget Fashionista.
>
> Study the list and all the possible failures that could occur. All of them, no matter how small they may seem to you.
>
> Then I want you to rip up this list and flush it down the toilet. Nothing in life is without risk, especially success. Sure, you might fail, but then you'll pivot. Then you'll fail again, and pivot again. It's okay. Remember, you got this.

Giving yourself the permission to fail also means giving yourself the permission to be vulnerable. We live in a world where the *perception* of perfection is often the goal, so we often avoid discussing the *path* to perfection. The famous photographer Keith Major, who has photographed some of the biggest stars in the world—including Beyoncé, Samuel L. Jackson, even President Clinton—once told me the difference between a great photographer and an okay photographer. It's not the type of camera or the years of art school. It's that a great photographer takes a thousand times more photos. They KNOW that most of them won't turn out, and they take more chances to capture something great.

Like most normal human beings, I've failed epically many times in my life. I've had enormous setbacks and times where all I wanted to do was fall into a pit with a super-comfortable pillow, my Company Store comforter, and an eighty-inch TV so that I could Netflix and cry for a week. However, it's from these failures that I had my greatest breakthroughs. *The Budget Fashionista* was created as a result of trying to channel the grief of my father dying into something other than shopping sprees at Nordstrom; digitalundivided was the result of a life-changing health scare that compelled me to think about leaving a personal legacy larger than how to score a Target coupon. Genius Guild was the result of living through the global COVID pandemic and the death of George Floyd, who was killed six blocks away from where I went to primary school.

Don't worry about failure impacting your future success. Some of the most famous white dude founders have failed so much that they've made it into an art form. And they STILL got investment. Travis Kalanick, serial entrepreneur and president emeritus of the Entitled White Dudes Failing WAY Up Club, narrowly steered his startup Scour away from a $250 billion lawsuit for alleged copyright infringement by declaring bankruptcy in October 2000. Less than six months later, he launched Red Swoosh, where he allegedly played fast and loose with employee withholdings for the IRS. After selling that venture for a tidy sum, he got billions of dollars of investment for Uber, including from the firm Benchmark—which sued him in 2017 for allegedly packing the board. AND, even after his spectacular flameout at Uber, he still walked away with $1.4 billion and got MORE money for his next venture, the investment fund 10100.

So act like an Entitled white dude and embrace failure as a part of the path to success. Yes, we Builders don't have many (or for some of us, any) passes, but what we do have is the ability to turn the lessons learned from the fights we've survived throughout our lives into the armor to fight for our success. Oh no, my founder friend, failing is not the end of success. No, failing is just the beginning. And it's important for a great founder.

The Ingredients of a Great Founder

"Success is where preparation and opportunity meet."* Preparation is a great way to reduce the risk and fear that come with being an entrepreneur. So what does it look like to be properly prepared for your entrepreneurial journey? Research by Thomas W. Y. Man and others identified three core areas that separate successful small and medium-sized companies from unsuccessful ones: Potential, Process, and Performance. I'd add a fourth: the ability to Pivot. Let's go over how these four areas apply to your startup.

1. Potential

There is an old saying that goes "Opinions are like assholes, everyone's got one." Well, it's also true of "great ideas." Yes, having an idea is the first step in building a great company, but your idea alone doesn't define your

---

*Paraphrasing ancient Roman philosopher Seneca, car-racing great Bobby Unser, who was like an uplifting quote machine, often said this to fellow drivers. Racing legend Willy T. Ribbs, who experienced a lot of racism in his career as one of the first Black drivers, stated that Unser once told him, "There's not a lot of drivers that could have done and handled what you do. I know, because I heard what people were saying." Ribbs credits this quote as the fuel that helped him continue to compete.

potential. In the business world, potential is about having the skills to execute your idea.

There are two general types of knowledge when it comes to building a company. Your domain knowledge is your educational and professional expertise in the specific field. Your social knowledge is your experience as a customer or recipient of a service or product. I might have a great idea for a shuttle service to Mars, but I'm not a rocket scientist, so my potential ability to build the shuttle is limited because I don't have the technical experience (domain knowledge) gained from working on other space missions and I'm also not a consumer of space shuttles (social knowledge).

You want to build businesses in an industry where you have, or can quickly acquire, the necessary domain knowledge and can utilize the help/experience of your existing network. This is especially true for a Builder's first company. This will give you the greatest potential for success because you will be able to build it faster (and cheaper) by utilizing existing resources.

A strong network, with years of domain experience as both an entrepreneur and investor, helped me to quickly raise millions for my company Genius Guild, a venture studio and venture capital fund that invests in startups led by diverse founders, before I even announced it publicly. I was able to hire a great staff from amazing people I met while building my other companies. Furthermore, I was able to quickly spot and solve challenges, like hires who weren't right for their roles, because I had experience managing these challenges before, something I talk about in detail in Step 5. I'm not saying you can't build a business in an industry you don't have a professional/educational background in; it will just be riskier. It may take longer and cost more money because you don't have the existing experience to understand what you're building (domain knowledge) or connections to the right people to help you (social knowledge).

The more knowledge and expertise you have in the industry you're trying to build your company in, the more likely you are to find success. You can call in favors with your colleagues and friends. You can gain introductions to potential clients, suppliers, and advisors through your personal and professional network.

For your first company, it's best to focus on an idea in an industry where you have as much experience as possible. Personal experience as a consumer is helpful, but there's a big difference between *receiving* a service and *giving* a service. For example, there's an enormous difference between eating at a restaurant and running your own. As a patron of the restaurant, you get to enjoy the amazing food, but you don't have the sliced fingers and dehydration of the chefs in the kitchen. You may fret a bit about the number on the check, but you don't have to worry about having enough cash to cover salaries.

If you have a great idea but you haven't spent any time working in the industry, you should seriously consider trying to find a co-founder, a partner who helps you build your company. There's a reason so many startups have two founders: one can handle the business and marketing side of things while the other focuses on technical knowledge of the product and industry. If you can't find someone from the industry to partner with and you have no experience in the industry, reconsider whether or not you want to build this idea.

2. Process

You have an awesome idea for a company in a field you've worked in for over twenty years. But do you know how to translate this idea into an actual company? Process is the series of systematic steps you need to go from idea to the business of selling a product. Imagining the next big thing isn't the same as creating it. If you really want to make your dream work, you have to know how to build it into a viable company.

Not all Builders are exactly the same. Some of us have a knack for breaking down the nitty-gritty steps of the process. Others have big-picture goals and a general outline. Both can make it, and both need to invest in partners who make up for what they lack. Devoting the time and energy to recruiting people for your team is critical, which is a big focus of Step 5. Even if you are process oriented in your work, a second pair of eyes always helps. And don't get defensive when they start poking holes in your process. Thank them for their time, revise your flowchart, and go show it to a couple more people. Rinse and repeat.

3. Performance

Performance, aka execution, is how well your company or product competes in the market once built. Remember, someone has probably thought of your idea already—there are very few new ideas out there. So the difference between the other person's idea and your idea is going to be based on how well you're able to build and promote yours. This is where you can make or break your startup.

As you start to plan and build your product, strive for excellence every step of the way to set yourself apart. This means having high standards for your partners and employees, and even higher standards for yourself. This is *your* dream, don't shortchange it.

While having high standards is important in building your company, don't let perfection be the enemy of progress. As you will learn in Step 4, the early versions of your product/company will be the furthest things from perfection. And that is very okay. What helps maintain high standards is prioritizing the experience of your stakeholders and customers. How are they experiencing your product, and how can their experience be better? When you think like them, you'll deliver a product experience fine-tuned to their needs and desires.

AND...

4. Pivot

One of the biggest keys to entrepreneurial success is a willingness to abandon an idea that isn't working and shift course toward something that shows more promise—the ability and the will to pivot. There are many famous stories of companies that completely changed direction early on. For instance, YouTube was originally launched as a dating site where users could post videos describing their ideal partner. Twitter rose from the ashes of a platform for podcasting called Odeo. Groupon was initially built as a platform called the Point where people could form communities to support causes they were passionate about. All of these companies (and many more) changed direction when they realized their business wasn't working.

The ability to view failure as an opportunity to pivot, rather than as a sign you aren't talented, is what Stanford psychologist Carol Dweck calls a "growth mindset." Insecurity and a fear of failure are natural feelings, but giving in to them inhibits your ability to build a successful company. This lesson is particularly important for Builders to internalize, as we're likely to encounter many roadblocks along the path to success.

Builders with a growth mindset are able to navigate the ambiguity of entrepreneurship and turn that ambiguity into a solid enterprise. When things aren't working, they change their strategy and try something new. Imagine the business world as a deep, dark forest. People with a growth mindset can create a path through the forest. If it leads to a dead end, they can quickly envision a new one. Conversely, those with a fixed mindset won't be able to envision a new way through the forest. Be willing to carve new paths. When something isn't working, don't give up. Pivot to something new.

The Five Bald-Faced Lies Told to Builders

It can take a lifetime to sort through all the truly horrible advice you'll be told as you create your startup. Often these opinions are stated as facts, until someone proves them to be myths. For example, before 2014, the idea was that you simply couldn't build a successful startup outside of Silicon Valley. The head of a very well-known venture firm once told me that they loved the work I was doing with the social enterprise I founded to increase the number of high-growth companies founded by Black women, but they wouldn't fund us unless we moved from New York (Black population: 24.3 percent) to Silicon Valley (Black population: 2.3 percent). Fast-forward five years: extremely successful companies like the e-commerce platform Etsy (New York) and the fintech platform Kabbage (Atlanta), and funds like Steve Case's Rise of the Rest, which focus solely on investing in startups located outside Silicon Valley, have shown that tech can thrive in the rest of the United States. Companies like Spotify (Sweden), Gojek (Indonesia), and WeTransfer (the Netherlands) show that startups thrive globally.

As a Builder, you will need to develop the ability to separate fact from opinion. Entitleds have a habit of sharing information that they literally pulled out of thin air as if it's fact. They get away with doing this because so few of us have run this race that there's no one fact-checking them. It's important to do your own fact-checking. Here's some of the truly horrendous, stupid, idiotic "advice"—aka lies—I was given while building my business.

LIE 1:
You MUST Know How to Code to Build a Startup

Don't know how to code? Well, neither do 99.9 percent of the tech venture capitalists and a surprising number of startup founders. When I first started *The Budget Fashionista*, I didn't know how to code either, but I still managed to turn a little blog into a viable company and a successful exit.

No, you don't *need* to know how to edit an SQL database[*] in order to create a successful startup. However, if you're building a tech-enabled company, it will be helpful to know a bit of code. It's very hard to operate in a community if you can't speak the language. You don't need to rush out and take a coding class, but until low-code and no-code software[†] become completely ubiquitous, it's in your best interest to know enough to be able to communicate with your developer. Think of it this way: when you go on vacay to a non-English-speaking country, you try to learn a little of the language in order to get around. Think of learning at least a basic amount of code as a way to help you communicate within the startup community.

Now, before you panic and abandon your startup idea because coding scares you, it's important to note that coding *isn't* that hard! Tech bros have built up this idea that coding takes genius-level knowledge and skill, but it really doesn't. Big tech likes to act like coding is a skill unattainable

---

[*]This is the standard language for relational database management systems.
[†]Low code (little code is needed to build the software) and no code (which means exactly that: no code needed to build the software) are options we will discuss in Step 4: Product-Market Fit: How to Turn Your Solution into a Money-Making Business. Tools like Zapier (low code) and Airtable (no code) are great for helping you build early versions of your company without hiring a developer.

to the average Builder, when in reality the tech bros have just made it seem that way in order to make themselves look (and feel) special. Coding is a skill like any other that you can learn through study and practice. Remember how we talked about using Entitleds' technological advances to level the playing field for Builders? Coding is a perfect example: thanks to the tech bros, there's an endless supply of online coding courses, many of them free!

Of course, there are advantages to knowing how to code. My husband, Tobias, is a software engineer for a major tech company, which means he knows how to build websites and applications. On any given week, he has four to five people pitching him ideas. Tobias and his developer friends don't need you, but *you* need *them*. It's much like how a contractor can build a house without an architect, but an architect can't build a house without a contractor. The rock stars in tech are those who can create something out of your ideas, which is why having a basic understanding of the computing language being used to build your business is so important.

Tobias's list of things he needs to build before he builds your idea

1. His wife's ideas
2. His employer's ideas
3. His ideas
4. His mom's ideas
5. His cousin's ideas

. . .

1,001,332. Your idea

THE TRUTH: CODING ISN'T THAT IMPORTANT, AND IT'S ALSO EASY TO LEARN

Sure, knowing how to code will be helpful if your startup heavily depends on software. But if you already know you're going to have a different role in your business, or perhaps are founding a business with very few advanced tech requirements, don't waste your time and energy panicking over coding. There are developers out there looking to partner with early-stage startups and, if you have the capital, you can hire them to take on your heavy coding work or convince them to join your team as co-founders (more on this in Step 4).

LIE 2:
You MUST Graduate from an Elite University

Startup people love to say that the best founders come from elite institutions like Harvard, MIT, and Stanford. What purveyors of this myth neglect to tell you is that a large number of funded startups come from these institutions because these also happen to be top schools attended by investors. They are taking the outcome of their limited networks and creating a *pattern* that reinforces the biases that exist in their networks. *I only recruit founders from Stanford . . . My best investments come from Stanford.* We've talked about this pattern-matching bias before. Pattern matching is a convenient and rational-seeming way to exclude groups of people from receiving venture capital support.

Yes, white men have generally been able to sell their startups more often than other groups in the past. But is this because white men are better at building startups or because investors have small networks and fewer women and minorities have the opportunity? (Hint: it's the latter.)

THE TRUTH: Most Successful Startup CEOs Did NOT Go to Elite Schools

Some of the world's most successful companies were founded by people *without* a degree from an elite institution, including a number of the rich white guy founders (cognitive dissonance is real). Jack Dorsey, co-founder of both Twitter and Square, went to Missouri University of Science and Technology. Steve Case, founder of AOL, went to Williams College, a small school in northern Massachusetts. And a number of famous founders didn't even complete college at all! Steve Jobs, god of tech bros, went to Reed College, a small liberal arts school in Oregon, then De Anza community college in Silicon Valley, but never graduated. Billionaire Richard Branson didn't go to any university. At all.

While it may seem like all startups are run by a bunch of geeky twenty-five-year-old Entitleds in Stanford hoodies, the truth is anyone can build a startup. In fact, the average age of a successful startup founder is forty-five. Tina Sharkey was fifty-three years old when she founded the consumer goods company Brandless in 2017. Though it raised over $300 million in venture investment, it closed in February 2020—then got a second chance in 2021 after raising a fresh $118 million. Beatriz Acevedo, founder of the Latinx media startup mitú, graduated from the University of California, San Diego. Many founders don't even have access to venture capital. Liberian-born Richelieu Dennis sold Sundial, a beauty company including brands like SheaMoisture targeted to Black customers that he co-founded with his mom on the streets of Harlem, to Unilever for $1.6 billion.

Amazing Founders Who Didn't Go to an Elite University

COMPANY	FOUNDER	SCHOOL(S) ATTENDED
Carol's Daughter	Lisa Price	City College of New York
mitú	Beatriz Acevedo	University of California, San Diego
YouTube	Steve Chen, Chad Hurley, and Jawed Karim	University of Illinois at Urbana-Champaign, Indiana University of Pennsylvania, University of Illinois at Urbana-Champaign
Apple	Steve Jobs	Reed College, De Anza College
Bad Boy	Sean "Puffy" Combs	Howard University
Twitter	Jack Dorsey	Missouri University of Science and Technology, New York University
Ruby Love	Crystal Etienne	Baruch College, City University of New York
WordPress	Matt Mullenweg	University of Houston

LIE 3: You MUST Follow the "Rules"

I once got a DM* from a leader of a diversity in coding group stating that we (meaning Builders) need to learn how to work the "system" and follow the rules in order to be successful in the startup space. It was an *interesting*† conversation because there's no indication that following the rules has been the path to success for Builders. If that was true, wouldn't the people who run the world look a lot more representative of the world itself? Following the rules has, at times, kept us safe, but it hasn't kept us wealthy.

THE TRUTH: Successful Entrepreneurs Give No Damns About "Rules"

Builders create their own rules. Often, diverse founders are told they should go "work for someone in the space" before they start their company. They're told to pay their dues and that they just need a bit more experience. Yet research indicates that previous work experience isn't actually much of a marker for success. Working for someone else might widen your network, but it doesn't mean you will build a successful company.

And the truth is, the Entitled white boys of tech don't ever follow that rule themselves. Larry Page and Sergey Brin, the founders of Google, didn't say, "Oh, let's go work at Microsoft before we build the most powerful company on the planet!" Mark Zuckerberg didn't think, "Once I graduate from Harvard, I'm going to go work for IBM and then start Facebook."

---

*Follow me on IG @hiiamkathryn.
†Not really.

STEP 1: GET YOUR MIND RIGHT

Just take Maria Contreras-Sweet, the former head of the Small Business Administration under President Obama, who broke the rules of how banks get funded. The daughter of meat packers, she founded ProAmerica Bank by getting her friends and family, many working-class folks, to invest funds from their 401(k) accounts, building the bank into one of the most successful commercial banks in the Latinx community.*

Big ideas are what lead to BIG companies. Small ideas don't change the world.† Knowing the system and following the rules is great—if you want to work for someone else.

LIE 4:
You MUST Build a Certain Type of Startup

When I was using technology to build the beauty brand for Black women, I was told by Voldemort the Venture Capitalist and his Death Eaters (fellow VCs) that (Black) beauty wasn't a "startup." In his mind, only Google could be a startup. Now internet-based beauty brands like Glossier, IPSY, and BROWN GIRL Jane are all well-known and successful beauty startups.

THE TRUTH: ANYTHING CAN BE A STARTUP

Literally anything can be a startup. Khaki pants for men? Yep, that's a startup (Bonobos). Eyeglasses? Warby Parker. Generic household products? Brandless. Top K-pop teen singing group factory? Bighit Music.‡

---

*She later led a group of investors to buy convicted sexual abuser Harvey Weinstein's The Weinstein Company.
†A small idea and a simple idea aren't synonymous. Many big ideas are actually quite simple, though their execution may be hard.
‡K-pop supergroup BTS became millionaires when Bighit, their label, went public on the South Korean stock market in 2020.

Don't believe every idea can be a startup? Here's a brief list of all the very non-techy ideas that are now well-funded startups.

THE IDEA	THE STARTUP
Cotton swabs	LastSwab
Khaki pants for dudes	Bonobos
Tampons and maxi pads	LOLA
Eyeglasses	Warby Parker
Hair weaves	Mayvenn
Venture capital	Genius Guild
Generic household products	Brandless
Preschool	Wonderschool
House paint	Clare
Virtual "big box" retail	Amazon
Luggage	Away
Insurance	Lemonade
Human resources	Gusto
Grocery shopping	Instacart
Dental floss	Cocofloss
Basic kids clothing	Primary
Makeup	Glossier

Khaki pants. Cotton swabs. Hair weaves. Dental floss. Yeah, everything is and can be a startup.

LIE 5:
You MUST Protect Your Idea from Thieves!

Every time I give a speech—EVERY TIME—at least one person will ask, "How do I protect my idea from getting stolen?" Our staff actually places bets on how long it will take before someone asks this question.*

Scared someone is going to steal your idea? Here's a foolproof way to protect your idea from thieves:

First, write your idea on a piece of paper. Do not share the idea or piece of paper with anyone, including your pet dog, your friends, or anyone who could help fund you or help you build the idea. Then, place the piece of paper with the idea in a safe that only you know the combination to.

Voilà, your idea is 1,000 percent protected! Yes, you won't be able to build it, get funding, or acquire customers, but at least it's safe and no one can steal it from you! You're a winner!

THE TRUTH: PROTECT YOUR IDEA BY BUILDING YOUR IDEA

The only way to protect your idea is to build it. It's useless just sitting in a vault or lying dormant in your mind. Building a business involves inherent risk, but you must be brave enough to build it. You owe it to yourself and that genius idea of yours. If you realize a version of your idea has already been built by someone else? Build it better.

---

*Usually by the third question.

Many people will tell you to get a trademark or a patent on your idea. Look, unless you have a cure for cancer or some amazingly inventive technology that *you can build yourself*, getting a patent or trademark at the start of your building journey is a total waste of money. A patent or trademark only protects you if you sue, and a lawsuit is costly. In America, patents cost between $1.6 and $3 million to litigate, according to the American Intellectual Property Law Association. Also, filing a patent lawsuit reduces the likelihood of potential investors wanting to work with you because of fear of being sued.

As an investor, I hear hundreds of pitches every year. The reality is I often don't understand how one company's Orange Thingy is different from everyone else's Orange Thingy. If a founder asks me to sign an NDA for something that is clearly not a high-tech idea, it raises red flags for me. Instead of hiring lawyers to draft all of these unnecessary documents they should be spending that money building the company.

You've Got Your Mind Right, and Now It's Time to Build

You've embraced your fears. You are now ready to build your personal toolbox, which will provide the foundation and tools to help you celebrate the peaks and valleys that will come with building a company.

You GOT this.

You're not a chicken. You're going to roll up . . . and you're going to be, like, "Bak, bak, bitch."

Peik Lin, the GOAT* of best friends from the movie *Crazy Rich Asians*

*GOAT = Greatest of all time

STEP 2

Your Personal Success Toolbox: How to Gather the Tools to Build Your Company

You just completed the first step in building a successful business, mentally preparing yourself. Now, it's time to create the internal tools you'll need to succeed, what I call your "toolbox."

When we talk about a personal success toolbox, we're not talking about a literal toolbox from your local hardware store. We're talking about the personal frameworks, processes, and strategies that you will refer to time and time again as you build your company. These differ from, say, your pitch deck, which is a very important business tool but not one that you use every day. A pitch deck, which we will discuss in more detail in later steps, is what you use to communicate your company to potential partners, customers, etc., and helps you secure the funds you need to build your company. A pitch deck, however, won't help you deal with the distant relative who just heard about the pitch contest you won and wants to "borrow" a few dollars. However, creating a personal advisory board and having them in your toolbox to help redirect that relative allows you to stay focused on building your business.

Tool #1: Start a Mindfulness Practice

I'm a huge fan of documentaries like *The Last Dance*, ESPN's compelling series about Michael Jordan and the 1990s Chicago Bulls. As I watched the series, I noticed that every time Michael Jordan stepped to the free throw line, he took a breath. It was a short breath, but a breath. After some reading, I discovered that "His Airness" worked with a breathing and meditation coach during his tenure as a basketball superstar. Breathwork, as it's called, is a core part of a mindfulness practice.

Michael Jordan took a breath to create a space between thinking and doing. That can seem counterintuitive as you build a business where you're rewarded for doing the absolute most. However, mindfulness is probably one of the most important tools you can develop to help you build your company, because that extra pause gives you the opportunity to get very clear about your next step. Jordan took the extra breath so that he could focus on sinking that free throw. Serena Williams takes a breath to focus before she releases her powerhouse serves. The late Supreme Court justice Ruth Bader Ginsburg would take a breath prior to delivering a groundbreaking opinion (or dissent) to focus her words.

Before you make a big decision, take a deep breath, hold it for the count of four, and then release it. When you are stressed, focus on taking a series of breaths. Sometimes it's helpful to have a mantra to say while you hold it in. As I breathe in I say the mantra "The world is conspiring for your greatness," and then I let the breath go. It takes all of about one second, but that one second gives me a chance to pause to reflect.

Tool #2: Name Your Price

At his October 2011 appearance on *Inside the Actors Studio*, the sometimes-*very*-problematic comedian Dave Chappelle recounted a conversation he'd had with his dad in 1991. Chappelle had just graduated from Washington, DC's famed Duke Ellington School of the Arts with plans to pursue comedy instead of going to college. His dad took him aside and said, "Name your price in the beginning. If it ever gets more expensive than the price you name—get outta there."

Fast-forward to 2004, when Dave signed a $50 million deal for a third and fourth season of *Chappelle's Show* on Comedy Central. But feeling very uncomfortable with the deal, he decided that price was in fact too high; he walked away.

Michaela Coel, the brilliant British television writer and actor who found a great deal of global success with her comedy series *Chewing Gum* on Netflix, turned down a $1 million deal from the platform for her next series. Why? The streaming platform was reluctant to give her ownership of her new series, *I May Destroy You*. For Michaela, ownership and creative control of the deeply personal series, inspired by her own experience being sexually assaulted, meant she would be able to shape how it was presented to the world. So Michaela left Netflix, fired her agents, and pitched the series herself. She eventually scored a deal with the BBC and HBO that gave her ownership and a seat at the table. She won an Emmy Award in 2021 for her writing for the series.

There will be a time in the process of building your business when you are going to be faced with a challenge to your integrity. It can be very expensive to have integrity when you're a Builder. As a CEO, I've faced a number of these challenges. In one particularly hard instance, it was an offer for a large amount of investment that also came with activities that compromised the integrity of the organization and my own personal integrity. Several millions of dollars were at stake, yet the price was just too high, so I walked away (slowly, because it was *game-changing money*). Less than two years later the organization received even more support without the questionable strings attached.

You will face a slew of other challenges—to your bank account, your personal life, even to your mental health. It's important to be very clear before you start to even build your company about the line you will not cross. Naming your price—recognizing your core values and defining what constitutes a violation of them—is crucial to building a successful company. These values are your own personal truths—the things you hold dear and are central to you as a person. They're your North Star that will help you define partnerships, make decisions about hiring and funding, and check yourself to make sure you're achieving your goals.

Creating a set of core values is fairly straightforward. Just open a doc or grab a sheet of paper and list all the actions, words, attributes that are important to you. Then begin to refine this list into a set of principles. Below is a list of my core values. I'm not saying your core values need to be as comprehensive as this, but generating a list of two to three central values is a great place to start.

Kathryn's Core Values

INTEGRITY

I model leadership by practicing integrity in my thoughts, my words, and my actions.

I strive to:
- Do what I say and say what I do
- Come prepared, be on time, and stay engaged
- Live in my truth

Empathy

I understand that everyone is fighting/winning a battle that I may not see.

I strive to:
- See the whole person
- Give space to myself and others to make mistakes (and to correct them)
- Give space to myself and others to win

Clarity

I am clear in my intentions, goals, and dreams.

I strive to:
- Acknowledge that my truth may not be your truth
- Share my expectations with others
- Be very clear in my communication

Fearlessness

I do the right thing, even when it's hard.

I strive to:

- Acknowledge that "what other people think about me is none of my business"*
- Be bold in my actions
- Leave the world a better place

Tool #3: Know Thyself

A few years back, I was having a discussion with a well-known investor and philanthropist in the tech space. This person hadn't invested in my organization, even though we fit directly into her mission and investment thesis of supporting women, especially diverse women. I really wanted to know why she didn't invest in our company.

Sometimes when you want to know the answer to a sticky question, the best way to get there is to get straight to the point. So I asked her why she didn't invest in us. She paused and then asked me, "Who are you?" Not in the snotty way of "Why are you asking me, a person of great wealth, this question?" Rather she was asking what I stood for (and, in turn, what the organization stood for).

At that moment, I could have given her a killer elevator pitch about *the enterprise*, but what I could not do was give an elevator pitch about *Kathryn*. I could give answers that were quite external to myself—I was a CEO, a mom, a wife—but I couldn't answer who I really was. At that moment, I realized that for many years I hadn't taken the time to define myself for myself. And not pausing for a moment to do so cost my organization millions of dollars.

---

*Amazing quote from a "friend in my head," RuPaul.

I literally didn't know who I was and as a result didn't know what my company was.

As an early-stage investor, I often don't have concrete business proof that the company I'm investing in will be successful. So I bet on the founder—or not. Investor Kathryn wouldn't have bet on then-entrepreneur Kathryn. The fact that I couldn't even define myself for myself didn't inspire confidence that I would have a clear vision for my company.

Use the work you did in your core values to create your personal mission statement: a basic answer to the question "Who am I?"

As the founder of your company, what you believe in and who you are is all you have. It's people who build companies, not ideas. And as the first employee you set the course for your company. What is it that you believe in? What is the statement that will be in your toolbox?

When I'm asked this question now, my personal mission statement is clear . . . I'm a builder.*

Tool #4: It's All About the SWOT

You need a clear understanding of what you're good at and what you aren't. This is a crucial component of getting yourself prepared to be a leader. Taking an honest, hard look at yourself will help you be able to anticipate where there may be some difficulties, so you're prepared to seek help. It will also uncover strengths that can be useful for you as you build your company.

The challenge with conducting self-assessments is that they are rarely

---

*Sometimes the best answer is also the simplest. Don't feel pressure to write a book about who you are.

completely accurate. Most of us rate our abilities and skill sets more highly than others rate them. However, self-assessment is still useful as a way to help you, the entrepreneur, think through how your strengths and weaknesses can impact your business. This analysis is a living document, so you can always be conscious of your skills and weak spots.

I like to use a Strengths, Weaknesses, Opportunities, and Threats (SWOT) analysis, a decision-making tool used by many consulting firms and corporate advisors, to conduct my personal assessments. We all have blind spots. Some of us are very aware of our strengths but tend to overlook our weaknesses. Others see threats everywhere but don't notice opportunities. The SWOT analysis forces you to think critically about all four areas so you can gain a realistic view of the factors that might help and hurt you.

The setup:
Draw a square and divide it into a two-by-two grid.
Label the squares "Strengths," "Weaknesses," "Opportunities," and "Threats." You will put your response to each of the four areas of the SWOT in their corresponding square.

Strengths (upper left box): What are your helpful characteristics or skills? Example: your strong analytical mind or talent for project management.

Questions to ask yourself as you build out your Strengths section:

- What are my top three strengths?
- What activities make me feel empowered?

- Review past job reviews or feedback. What do others say are my strengths?

Weaknesses (upper right box): What do you find difficult that might hold you back? Example: time management or your lack of knowledge of financial analysis.

Questions to ask yourself as you build out your Weaknesses section:

- What are situations that make me feel insecure?
- Review past job reviews or feedback. What do others say are my areas for improvement?
- What do I fail to do?
- What are my negative work habits?

Opportunities (bottom left box): The bottom left box is where you list external things that are helpful to you. Example: your school's active alumni network (potential customers!).

Questions to ask yourself as you build out your Opportunities section:

- What aspects of my company motivate me?
- Do I have or can I develop a strategic network to help me build my company?
- What industries or areas do I have unique insight into?
- Are there any family connections that might help me build my company?

> **Threats (bottom right box):** These are external things that could present challenges to you. Childcare problems, lack of flexibility at your nine to five—all can present roadblocks to your ability to build your startup.
>
> ### Questions to ask yourself as you build out your Threats section:
>
> - Are there any personal or family challenges that may make it difficult for me to build my company?
> - What weaknesses do my threats expose?
> - What strengths do my threats expose?
> - What are my current obstacles?

Tool #5: Create a Personal Advisory Board (PAB)

When most people think of building an advisory board or board of directors, they think of it in the context of their company. You look for advisors whose experience and LinkedIn connections can help your company grow. But your personal advisory board, the group of people you will turn to when you need advice, is a little different. It should be composed of people who want to see you win—not just your company—and they should feel open enough to be honest with you. This group shouldn't necessarily be your besties. While a few close friends or family members might be a part of this informal board, the people closest to us may often find it hard to tell us what we really need to hear in difficult situations.

Characteristics of Your Personal Advisory Board

The first step is to examine your personal SWOT analysis, especially your weaknesses and threats. Do you know anyone who can help you overcome these challenges?

For example, one of my threats are distant family members who pop up every time I do something very public, like win thousands of dollars on a TV game show.* These family members are very skilled at showing up just as the wired money clears and throwing as much Oscar-level drama as humanly possible. Therefore, my mom, who is an excellent cuckoo family member blocker, is a vital part of my personal advisory board. She blocks these challenges before they even reach me. And she is clear on her role as the blocker of drama. She has, to adapt lines from the movie *Taken*, "a very particular set of skills, skills she acquired over a very long career. Skills that make her a nightmare" for dramatic family members.†

The best board members are people you can trust to have your back and tell you what you need to hear, and they should be willing to travel every step of the journey of building your company with you.

Here are a few roles your board of advisors can play for you:

- **A BS Meter.** This person should have the ability to assess when you are not only being dishonest with them, but also when you are being dishonest with yourself. It's easy to delude

---

*I was a contestant on *Who Wants to Be a Millionaire* and won $65,000.
†Go watch the movie *Taken*, just to see Liam Neeson in that scene. Scary. But not as scary as a seventy-year-old Black grandmother saying those lines to you.

yourself and keep pushing forward with something that's clearly not working. You need someone perceptive who isn't afraid to call you out on your blind spots and wishful thinking.

- **Motivator.** Building the damn thing is HARD. There will be at least once (or twice) where you will want to throw in the towel, the laptop, and the adjustable desk and reclaim your free time (remember that?). You need someone in your corner who will give you the little pushes you need to keep moving forward.
- **Listener.** There will be times on your entrepreneurial journey when you need to vent (and vent . . . and vent). Having a good listener in your corner is important. Unlike your BS Meter and your Motivator, your Listener isn't there to point out your delusions or pump you up. Their job is to empathize with you and say you're doing a great job. This is the kind of person who pats you on the back or gives you a hug and makes you feel better.
- **Your Personal Comedian.** Laughter is so important to our emotional well-being. You need to make sure you have a personal comedian on your team. Note: This person doesn't have to be an adult. They could be a child in your life who just makes you smile, or even a beloved pet (go ahead and put Fido on your board). For me, it's my kindergarten-age son, whose questions ("Why do we have toenails") and original songs (with rap breaks), often about toilets, never fail to crack me up.

Make sure you're clear with each member of your PAB—okay, maybe not your dog—about the role that they play for you so they know how best to help you. Is their role to listen or to push you forward? Do you need them to bring a bit of levity or to help you be true to yourself?

STEP 2: YOUR PERSONAL SUCCESS TOOLBOX

Tool #6: Find Your Exit Number

There's a common belief that you must leave your nine to five in order to build your business. Sure, Entitleds can do that, because their median family wealth in the United States is $171,000. But for us Builders (Black American families have a median wealth of $17,100 and Latinx American families have a median wealth of $20,600), leaving our day jobs without some indication that our idea can support us is financial suicide.

Before you peace out of your nine to five and tell your boss where they can go on a burning hot vacation, take a moment to figure out your exit number. Your exit number is the amount of money your business needs to make each month in order for you to be able to leave your day gig without putting your financial future at risk.

Note: Your nine to five (or the day job of someone close to you) can also provide crucial resources to help you build your business.* When we were building *The Budget Fashionista*, I was able to quickly upload photos to my site by using the ultrafast T1 lines at Tobias's office (much more efficient than the dial-up connection we had at home back then). Later on, the relationships I built at *TBF* helped me kick off digitalundivided with things like free space for events and sponsorships.

A word of caution: This exercise is to understand what you *really* need to be the best you. This number isn't what you need to live like Oprah. It's the amount you require each month to cover your basic necessities plus

---

*Make sure to double-check your employment agreement/contract with legal counsel as many have clauses that state your employer may own anything you produce while working for them.

a few extras.* Your business will need to support you at this level for at least a year without you dipping into your savings and retirement accounts.

I can't give you an exact number or formula here because what you need to get you through the day, week, or month is deeply personal. Some people need only a futon and cheese sandwiches to live. Others need a plush mattress and green juice. Private school for your kids might be a luxury for some but a necessity for others. Going to the gym every day may help you stay focused, while singing in your community choir may be the creative outlet you need.

Marie Kondo your budget. Ask yourself, "Does this item spark joy?" If not, let it go. Every book on budgeting tells you to get rid of lattes without asking whether lattes are the thing that gets you through the day. What if your latte is the only treat you are able to give yourself and it helps you to look at the day more optimistically? What if the coffee shop is the place where you connect with your community?

All of these tools will be extremely important in the next step, as you translate your idea into a solution that solves a problem.

You GOT this.

---

*Maslow's Hierarchy of Needs outlines a theory of human motivation whereby people cannot operate at higher functions without first meeting the basic needs of the underlying level. So, for example, at the base of the pyramid is physiological needs such as food, water, shelter, etc., and just above that is the need for security and safety.

What makes you think that's the best of me?

Mariah Carey, in one of the greatest movies of all time, *Glitter*

STEP 3

You're NOT Your Customer: How to Make Sure Your Business Solves a Problem

Businesses, whether it's your corner shop or cloud server provider, solve problems. People pay businesses to solve a problem. A great idea alone isn't enough to build a successful business. You need an idea that solves a problem so well that a meaningful number of people will pay for your solution. This is the foundation of the market-based economy we live in.

For example, I *could* grow my own food, but I have limited time, space, and patience, so I pay the grocery store to solve this problem for me. I *could* cut my own hair. However, my hairdresser does a significantly better job than I would, so I pay her to cut my hair. During the COVID-19 pandemic, I homeschooled my son. However, teaching kindergarteners isn't a skill set that I possess, so I gladly paid his school to take over again as soon as I could.*

Case in Point: So Who Invented the Desktop Interface?

Most people think it was Microsoft or Apple that actually invented the desktop interface, the way your computer screen is organized like items on a desk. However, it was researchers at Xerox who actually invented the desktop interface (called a graphical user interface, or GUI) for its Alto personal computers in 1973; Steve Jobs and Apple saw the market potential for the desktop idea, made a few changes, and implemented it in their next operating system, the Lisa OS. Around this time Bill Gates was hanging at a tech trade show and saw VisiCorp's Visi On, which inspired him to develop an early version of Microsoft Windows. Eventually, this became the backbone for Windows 95, which reportedly sold 7 million copies in its first five weeks.

Every great business starts with a great idea. But, more importantly, that idea must address a problem that people are willing to pay for a solution to. In the 1970s, few people outside of universities had access to computers, so having an easy-to-use interface wasn't as much of a problem as figuring out which polyester pants suit to wear to the local disco. The GUI wasn't a solution people were willing to pay for at the time. In 1995, however, personal computers were becoming more accessible to

---

*Of the many things the pandemic taught us, one major thing was the importance of teachers. What is "new math" and what was so wrong with the old version? I'm going to get "Carry the One" tattooed on my arm. #LongLiveOldMath.

STEP 3: YOU'RE NOT YOUR CUSTOMER

the mass market and computer companies needed a way to make the devices easy to use. Computers with GUI became hot.

Ideas are extremely important when you're building a business. There would be no Windows 95 (and maybe even no Microsoft) if Xerox hadn't invented the GUI. If customers aren't willing to pay a premium for your product, then what you're building isn't a company, it's a hobby.* People weren't looking for a better personal computing experience in 1973, but they were in 1995 and were willing to pay for it.

As a Builder, the quicker you can get from your idea to the actual problem your business is trying to solve, the better. And the quicker you understand that a problem for you (or those in your closest circle) may not be a problem for everyone, the quicker you can find a bigger problem to solve. Your idea is important to *you*, but not to *me*. It becomes important to me when the idea you're building solves my problem. The problem you solve doesn't necessarily have to be super grand, like saving the world. It could be as simple as "I need a babysitter" (Care.com, founded by Filipino American Sheila Marcelo).

An Idea Searching for a Problem

In 2002, my dad, Bob, passed away. In most families, when you have someone dear who passes away, you mourn and you process it. You might

---

*I define "premium" as the cost to produce the goods/service plus a percentage over the costs to build the product/service for profit (also called profit margin). A quick Google search will give the average profit margins for major industries. This is very helpful in determining whether your idea can be a business or just a hobby.

experience depression or anger or just sadness. It usually causes you to pause for a moment to reassess your own mortality.

When my father passed away, my mom and brother and I decided to start a laundromat/dry-cleaning business in my hometown of Minneapolis. Why dry cleaning? Why not? For some reason we thought this was a great idea. In hindsight it was probably the dumbest thing we could have done. A grieving family starting a business in a highly regulated field in which we had absolutely no experience?

Ummm. Okay.

I now recognize that it was a way to put off dealing with the pain of my father's death. But back then, in the moment, it seemed like a truly brilliant idea. We had the capital (provided by my mom), we had the knowledge of our neighborhood and community, and we had the time. In my case, I had just left my job as an international epidemiologist, since having a terminally ill parent made it very difficult to travel to places like Sharm el Sheikh, Egypt,* and Jaipur, India.

However, it quickly became apparent that this wasn't the best idea.

My mom was still deep in mourning. I was getting married later that year and lived a thousand miles away in Philadelphia. My brother had a toddler and a new baby on the way. In addition to the grief (and avoidance thereof), there was A LOT going on in our family.

Too much . . . way too much to start a business.

The business person in me now wants to scream at young Kathryn and her poor family: Girl, don't hire a former CEO of IKEA and the former CEO of David's Bridal as consultants for a business they know nothing about. In fact, don't hire consultants AT ALL. Instead, block off a few weekends and go stand outside a laundromat/dry cleaner and interview actual customers.

---

*Sharm el Sheikh is a stunning resort town located on the Sinai Peninsula right on the Red Sea. I was scheduled to jump on a plane to present research at a conference there the day my father died.

Do they care about cleaner facilities or is convenience more important to them? Watch how they use the facilities and services. Would the additional cost of tech add enough utility* for customers to pay higher prices?

So the business failed. Like, really failed. My mother lost over seven figures. Yeah, you read that right. It was a big, costly mistake that made a major impact on the entire family, far beyond just my mom, my brother, and me. You know those local TV consumer reporters who expose bad businesses that supposedly do bad to their customers? Guess whose laundromat was featured? They literally sent a television crew to my brother's home to "collect" the clothing of customers. It was horrible and it almost ruined our family.

The failure of the dry cleaners caused a huge rift in my family. I had just lost my father. My brother and I were arguing all the time. I would spend days wandering the King of Prussia mall, and shopping was kind of where I went to just sort of pass the time and relieve stress. I couldn't save my family's business, but I could buy a fabulous pair of Gucci sandals. I had no friends—all my friends lived in New York City. I was lonely.

I made the decision that I would rather have my family than fight for a business that no one, including the people working on it, wanted.

So I left with my sanity and my relationship with my family intact.

The Four Steps to Defining Your Idea

What I learned from the failure of my family's dry-cleaning business is that great ideas that turn into great businesses solve problems. Focus on

---

*Aka value.

the *problem* your idea solves and whether this problem is big enough that people will pay for a solution. But how do you figure out whether your idea does this?

Tool: Translating Your Idea into a Problem to Solve

You have an idea (or two, or three). Awesome. Write it/them down.

"My idea is _____."

Take a look at the sentence you just wrote. Notice how the statement above centers around you as an entrepreneur? **Your goal as a Builder is to go from "idea" to "solution" in order to solve a problem for your customer.** We need to translate your idea from a you-focused statement into a customer-focused statement.

So how do you translate your brilliant idea into a solution people will pay for? By asking yourself the following questions:

1. Is my idea a problem looking for a solution or a solution looking for a problem? **Is it a real pain point?**
2. Is this a problem everyone has or just me? **Is this scalable?**
3. How is it currently solved, and do people pay for the solution? **Can I sell it?**
4. How often do they pay for the solution? **Can I get repeat customers?**

1. Defining the Pain Point

Is Your Idea a Problem Looking for a Solution or a Solution Looking for a Problem?

A problem is something that causes a person annoyance. In the startup world, such a problem is called a "pain point." Like the term "pain in the ass," I'm not talking about literal pain, but more figurative pain. Is your idea a solution to someone's pain in their ass?

> **Tool: Use Twitter to Find Out If Your Idea Is a Pain Point**
>
> A quick way to find out whether your idea is truly solving a problem is to just do a quick search of Twitter. Why Twitter? Because the shorthand nature of Twitter has made it the de facto customer service hotline of the world. If you see lots of people complaining about something, you can be confident that others have this painful problem.

2. Finding the Scale of the Problem

Is This a Problem Everyone Has or Just Me?

Maybe you have an *awesome* idea to solve a *huge* problem, but it's only a problem for you or a few people in your circle. Finding the scale of the problem, and, in turn, the number of people who might be interested in buying your solution, is a crucial part of starting your company (we'll dive deeper into this in the next step).

If it's not scalable, you won't be able to find enough customers to make a profit. This is why your early online research is crucial for determining whether you have a real shot at turning your idea into a profitable company.

In business, you either go BIG or you go broke. Using the information you gathered from your Twitter searches, try to get even more information on the scale of the problem you are planning to solve by using the Google Trends tool (https://trends.google.com) to see how many people are searching for information on terms associated with your idea. The tool, based on a scale of 0 (little data/no interest, e.g., "Kerri Kordashian") to 100 (high interest/peak popularity, e.g., "Kim Kardashian"), shows how popular a term is relative to all the other searches in a given geographic area.

So what's a good baseline to indicate the strength of interest in your idea? I use at least three incidences of a popularity of at least 25 over the past six months on the Google Trends chart.

3. Will People Pay for Your Solution?

How Is It Currently Solved, and Do People Pay for the Solution?

There are times when the pain point and scale of the problem are clear, yet people still don't want to pay for a potential solution. For example: public transportation in certain urban areas. Sure, having good public transit may reduce traffic and alleviate climate concerns, but in car-centric cities, people may not see the utility of the public option because they all have private means of transportation. The only way you can make money as a Builder is if you find a painful enough problem that many people are willing to pay for your solution.

The question of whether people will pay for a solution is tricky for Builders, mostly because until recently we weren't allowed to participate in a market-based economy. The value of our businesses, our wages, even our ability to sell products were suppressed by external forces.

It's hard to compete in the larger market when the cost of raw materials and even the valuation of property is set by society's perception of your value based on your identity. For example, homeownership is one of the primary paths to wealth creation in the United States. However, homes in America owned by Black people are often appraised at a lower valuation than homes owned by white people in the same neighborhood. The lower appraisals have resulted in an estimated $156 billion in cumulative losses for Black homeowners.

What this challenge, what at Genius Guild we define as a market inefficiency (a true understatement), means to you as a Builder is that you will need to do even more research to ensure you have data to counteract any biased perceptions that might impact your ability to solve the problem. For example, while in the incubator-where-ideas-go-to-die, I spent hours at the business library in New York gathering data from industry sources on Black hair. I created a document that had every industry stat available on Black hair, which I kept with me when meeting with any potential investor.

Doing this extra research is crucial for your company's success. You need to be prepared to rebut the Entitleds' prejudices and fill in the gaps in their knowledge when they try to dismiss your idea (which they *will*).

4. Getting Repeatable Customers

How Often Do They Pay for the Solution?

Most successful startups focus on a repeatable problem, or a pain point that people need a solution to more than once. The more frequently people experience a certain pain point, the more often they will need to buy your solution and the more money you will make per customer. If you create a solution people need for only a short time, make sure you've found a problem they will pay a high premium for or that there are enough customers to maintain a steady flow of business. For example, take the need for breastfeeding equipment. On the individual level, solving the problem of helping mothers pump breast milk for later use is repeatable for only a relatively short time. However, there are several million babies born each year, and many women have multiple children, so the large scale of the problem offsets its limited customer repeatability.

My family's idea for modern urban dry cleaners/laundromat wasn't a bad idea. There are around 29,500 laundromats in the United States, and these small businesses contribute nearly $5 billion to the U.S. economy. The laundromat business hadn't changed in fifty years, even though technology available to owners has changed quite a bit. New technologies like using cards instead of coins and front-loading machines that reduce water usage were increasing profit margins for laundromat owners. While technically having clean clothing isn't a "need" like water or food, it's definitely pretty basic on Maslow's pyramid. At some point, everyone has to clean their clothing (scale) and at a fairly weekly or biweekly frequency (repeatable customer). Some can purchase a washer and dryer, but it might not be possible structurally if you live in an apartment (pain point). Or maybe you just hate doing laundry like most of us do (major pain point).

Here're some great ideas that startups have translated into successful companies.

Idea: Period Panties

The definition of hell is to be away from home on a particularly heavy period day and ruin a good pair of underwear. It's a problem (pain point) that every one of the 800 million (scale) people menstruating each day have had at least once in their lives, and most would gladly pay for an effective solution to it. It's a recurring pain (repeatable customer) that remains as long as a person menstruates, and you have no choice but to purchase protection (sale). And it's a global problem (scale) that a number of startups (Ruby Love, Thinx, LOLA) are working to solve.

Idea: Outsourced HR

Globally, there's an estimated 213 million small businesses. There are 30.2 million small businesses in the United States, which employ close to 59 million people. This means they all have to run payroll (scale). Prior to the internet, running payroll as a small business owner was a tedious task controlled by a small group of payroll processors who charged high fees and provided little to no support on other HR-related tasks (pain point). Yet, legally, payroll has to be run at a consistent interval (repeatable customer), and millions of companies run payroll each week/month (sale). A number of startups (Gusto, Justworks) now serve as outsourced HR for these small businesses and run their payroll, as well as performing other HR tasks.

> **Builder Trap: My Idea Doesn't Solve a Problem**
>
> If your idea doesn't solve a problem that people other than your friends and family are willing to pay a premium for you to solve, it isn't a business, it's a hobby. I know this can be hard to hear when you feel like you have the world's greatest idea. Repeat after me: Making money in business isn't about what *you* want, it's about what *customers* want.

So let's see what it looks like to translate an idea to a problem statement, and a problem statement to a solution.

Example Startup: Terry's Taco Truck

After many years toiling away in the corporate world, you've decided to follow your dreams and start a taco food truck. You feel in your gut that it's a great idea, and all your friends and family love your tacos.

Great, but this is an *idea*, not a problem. We need to turn your idea into a problem statement, then we'll turn the problem statement into a solution (aka your new startup). The key to writing a powerful problem statement is to flip the perspective from you to the customer. For example:

"I want to start a taco truck."

vs.

"The community doesn't have anyplace to get fresh tacos."

You can see how this translates the statement from focusing on your desire to run a taco business to your community's need for fresh tacos.

Note that just because you frame your idea as a problem, you won't know if it's a problem that others will pay for until you test it. We'll explore how to do this in the next step.

It's crucial that you shift your mindset away from your own desires and focus on the needs of your customers. Frankly, what you want doesn't matter when it comes to running a successful business selling to strangers. This is why family and friends are often the worst people to seek advice and feedback from. Most of them want to see you succeed and win, so they might be willing to overlook things in order to encourage

STEP 3: YOU'RE NOT YOUR CUSTOMER

you. People with no personal connections to you won't overlook your flaws just to make you feel better. They will use your product if it solves a problem for them, and they won't if it doesn't.

Now use the work we did in this step to draft the first version of your elevator pitch (the brief description of your business that you'll give to people when you first meet). You can use the questions in the toolbox below to help you translate these answers into a solid pitch you can use when talking to potential investors or partners.

Tool: Drafting Your Elevator Pitch

Fill in the following blanks regarding your startup. Remember to *always start with the problem you are solving*.

The problem I'm solving is_____
_____.

The idea I'm building is_____
_____.

This is a problem for_____
_____.

The problem occurs this often _____
_____.

The customer currently solves this problem by_____
_____.

Customers currently pay $_____ to solve it.

Elevator pitches for ideas presented earlier in the chapter might look like this:

Period panties: *800 million people menstruate every day and can spend up to $160 per year on inferior menstrual products like maxi pads and tampons that destroy their clothes and create discomfort. I've created period-proof undergarments that save customers both money and clothes.*

Clean clothes: *Millions of Americans spend about $5 billion per year at dirty stinky public laundromats because they don't have an in-home solution to clean dirty clothes. My idea is to build clean, tech-enabled laundromats with high-powered washing and drying machines.*

Outsourced HR: *Small businesses make up 99.9 percent of all U.S. companies. Many of them find managing their payroll onerous and costly to complete on their own, with close to half paying more than $5,000 a year for HR management. I created a company that efficiently handles payroll and other tedious HR tasks so owners can focus on scaling their businesses.*

And the elevator pitch for our taco truck?

Americans eat 4.5 billion tacos every day, yet there's no restaurant that serves tacos within a ten-mile radius of our city center. The only option available for taco lovers is to make them at home or travel thirty miles to the nearest town, spending money on gas, in addition to four dollars per taco. My company, Terry's Taco Truck, is a local food truck that serves delicious tacos to our community.

STEP 3: YOU'RE NOT YOUR CUSTOMER

You've just translated your brilliant idea into a global problem. Give yourself a hug. Take a big, big breath. Go get a tall, cool glass of sparkling water. Now review your personal mission statement and core values, because they are about to be tested in our next step!

Remember, you GOT this.

Make more than the guys you thought you wanted to be with.

Cardi B, the resident philosopher of Instagram

STEP 4

Product-Market Fit: How to Turn Your Solution into a Money-Making Business

The holy grail of a great business is when a great solution meets a great market, aka product-market fit. Determining product-market fit is very helpful in making sure that what you're building is something people want to purchase. Often entrepreneurs confuse the fact that there's a market for their product with the market wanting your product. Yes, there is a market for amazing art, but that doesn't mean that the market *wants* my stick drawings. Ford wasn't the first car company, but their Model T was the one that the market adopted at scale, because it fit the needs of the market.

The Product-Market Fit Road Map: Build. Measure. Learn. Repeat.

First introduced by author Eric Ries in 2011 in his seminal book, *The Lean Startup*,* Build-Measure-Learn is a cycle, or feedback loop, through which your startup gains knowledge on the relationship (or lack thereof) of your product to your target market. You start the B-M-L loop by building the easiest, quickest version of your product: the Minimal Viable Product, or MVP. The only way to really test whether or not your solution fits your market is to create an early version of your product (Build) and put it into the market and record/observe its feedback through a process called "customer discovery" (Measure). Then you record all the feedback and observations you've uncovered from being in the market (Learn). These learnings are implemented in the next, improved version of your product, which starts the cycle again.†

In order to get your company to product-market fit, you have to be open (and vulnerable) to feedback that may contradict your beliefs about your business and your customer. Trust me, I know this sounds scary

---

*While there's a lot of information about the Build-Measure-Learn feedback loop available online, I strongly suggest adding *The Lean Startup* to your library as it's a really helpful tool in getting to product-market fit.

†One question that often comes up is how many B-M-L cycles you should do. The answer is that as a company, you are always doing the cycle as it's the only way to get close to perfect product-market fit. For example, software companies like Microsoft are always releasing updated versions of their software. These updates are the result of going through a B-M-L loop. What does change is who may be leading the B-M-L cycle. As your company gets larger, other team members, like your chief technology officer, may lead the process.

STEP 4: PRODUCT-MARKET FIT

(well, it *is* scary). There's a tendency for startup founders to *think* we know what our customers want, especially those of us who developed our businesses because of a personal need. As the founders of the wildly successful barbershop management tool Squire found out, that's not always the case.

Startup Story: How Squire Connected Barbershops to Their Customers

Let's rewind to 2015. Two young Black entrepreneurs, Songe LaRon and Dave Salvant, saw enormous potential in a virtually untapped market. They wanted to develop an app that made bookings and payments easier for barbers and their patrons. Barbershop management was exceedingly outdated. To get an appointment, you had to text/call/page* your barber and then wait for them to text you/call/find a pay phone to call you back. Or, if you had hours to kill, you could also just head down to the shop and wait until your barber was available.

Now, in the Black community a good barber is *essential*. You don't just let anyone do your hair. The fact that the Silicon Valley crew hadn't tapped into this need to bring barbershops into the digital age was woeful but unsurprising—but, as LaRon and Salvant saw it, it was also an incredible opportunity to bring their solution to a market with an obvious need and low competition. It was a no-brainer.

*Yes. There're still barbers with pagers.

The two entrepreneurs started their app: Squire, a nationwide booking and payment platform that helped barbershops manage their clientele and connect with new customers. While they first focused on the community that they knew, Black men, they had a plan to scale to serve barbers in all communities.

The founders first started out building an app for customers, based on their experience as customers (Build). Remember, there's a BIG difference between receiving the service and giving the service. The app gained little traction with barbershop owners (Measure). Squire soon learned that the primary customer needed to be barbershop owners, not barbershop clients, but they didn't have the necessary experience to understand the challenges of shop owners (Learn). The product was failing.

It's hard to reach product-market fit if you don't have clarity around the problem that your business is trying to solve. The Build-Measure-Learn cycle is the road map that will give you the clarity you need. After several years of trial and error, Squire's founders decided the only way to truly understand the challenges of barbershop owners was to own a shop (Build, *again*). So LaRon and Salvant used their life savings to buy a barbershop and get firsthand experience in the challenges of managing a shop. Buying a barbershop might seem a bit extreme, but it did give the founders crucial domain knowledge. They also took a step back and did hundreds of interviews with barbers (Measure, *again*), asking probing questions about how they manage their shops and gaining firsthand knowledge of the daily problems they face, like managing missed appointments and processing payments (Learn, *again*), in their customer discovery process (we will talk about this more later in the chapter).

The result of working through the Build-Measure-Learn loop? Squire developed their app into an important tool that made it more efficient for the estimated sixty thousand (scale) barbershops in the United States to manage appointments with their customers, reducing missed appointments (pain point) through a mobile-based app. An average of 20 percent of a barber's appointments are missed, so this is a frequent problem (repeated) that eats into their revenue (sale), since a missed appointment means lost time in which another client could have been scheduled. Squire serves as a point-of-sale app, allowing customers to pay for services directly via the app. The business makes money by charging a monthly fee to barbershop members based on the size of their shop.

According to one of their investors, ICONIQ Growth, going through the B-M-L cycle has led the company to enormous success. Squire has filed over $100 million worth of payments for over a thousand barbershops. Squire filled a gap that desperately needed to be filled for the Black market, and they made a lot of money in the process. LaRon and Salvant raised over $300 million from traditional venture funds like Trinity Ventures as well as celebrities like Stephen Curry and Pharrell Williams. Today, their company is valued at close to $1 billion.

Build: Building Your First MVP

The goal of an MVP is to spend *as little of your resources (time, money) as possible* building your initial product. Why do you want to spend as little as possible? Again, what you *think* your market wants and what it actually buys are most likely not the same thing. Unless you're Jeff Bezos, you probably don't have money to waste on building something people don't want. A good rule of thumb is to take 10 percent of the monthly exit number you calculated in Step 2 and use this as the max amount you can spend on your MVP. For example, if your exit number is $2,000 per month, the max you can spend on your first MVP is $200.

Your MVP could be as simple as an idea on a napkin, a PowerPoint presentation, or a landing page created using a WYSIWYG* site builder. The goal is to get enough of your idea translated from your head/elevator pitch to something that someone else can directly interact with to *start* testing out product-market fit.

Using MVPs to refine our idea is extremely important for the 99.9 percent of us without trust funds because any money we're spending developing our idea is money that we're taking away from our own pockets. It helps to "derisk" the process of building a business, so if this one idea fails it doesn't ruin your personal financial future. You'd rather be out $200 than $20,000 if your idea doesn't work. You can't know whether or not your idea is a business until you get feedback from people who are actually willing—or not—to buy your product.

Gone are the days when founders could just raise $$$$ based on a drawing on a napkin or an amazing pitch deck. But what you can get from that napkin (or PowerPoint in my case) is feedback to get to the next Build. Building an MVP is a process, meaning you will create several different versions of your MVP—each version a bit better than the next, until you have the final product. The challenge for you, my dear founder, is to make sure your MVP is advanced enough to get real feedback, but simple enough to require little to no cash.

---

*Squarespace, Wix, and WordPress are all WYSIWYG.

STEP 4: PRODUCT-MARKET FIT

First Step MVPs

IF YOUR END RESULT IS . . .	THEN TRY THIS AS AN MVP
Content site (web magazine, blog, etc.)	A free version using a content management system/tool like Medium, WordPress, or Substack
Physical product (hardware, gadget)	Clay model or hand-drawn images
Software (mobile app, software as a service)	Simple landing page of how product will work

Startup Story: How I Built My First MVP for digitalundivided

I learned the importance of a good MVP when building digitalundivided, a social enterprise focused on supporting Black women entrepreneurs.

After I sold The Budget Fashionista in 2013, I started working for a women-led startup named BlogHer. In 2006, when the company was founded, advertisers often dismissed the impact female influencers and bloggers had on driving business. Being called a "mommy blogger" was seen as an insult. BlogHer helped "mommy bloggers" and other women bloggers and influencers get paid for their work and brought awareness to the power of women online. The company was founded by three incredible women—Lisa Stone, Elisa Camahort Page, and Jory Des Jardins—who met at a blogging conference that was pretty much all dudes. They decided to create their own conference exclusively for women, which grew to an eight-figure business with a roster of thousands of women bloggers and influencers and raised funding from top venture investors like Comcast Ventures.*

The idea of helping other women secure the bag really appealed to me. At that time, a website could still make two to three dollars per CPM for those banner adverts on their sites.† Other platforms like Instagram were emerging that were ripe for brand collaborations. I knew I could use my experience building the TBF business to help other women build their businesses as well.

My role at BlogHer was to expand the company's presence in the lifestyle space. I was essentially an influencer of influencers. I also worked to bring current and upcoming media superstars into the organization as partners, increasing the amount of ad inventory the company could sell and help women entrepreneurs to monetize their content. I loved the eclectic BlogHer community and found myself becoming friends with other influencers like Ree Drummond, aka the Pioneer Woman, and Luvvie Ajayi. As a result of my role and connections at BlogHer, I spoke and repped the company at conferences—including many in Silicon Valley.

Now, even though it was 2012, it was like 1912 in Silicon Valley. There were little to no women, yet alone any Black women, in the startup world. At one popular conference in San Francisco, I counted twenty-five women out of two thousand attendees. There were so few women that men had to wait in line for the restroom, while we few women easily breezed in without waiting. We gave one another virtual high-fives every time we passed.

---

*I was drawn to BlogHer's legendary conference attended by 5,000+ influencers, where each year McDonald's built a virtual restaurant within the party. The fast-food restaurant would set up fry stations inside ballrooms and have tables piled high with free cheeseburgers. Imagine all-you-can-eat hot McDonald's fries. Also, as I later learned once I became a mom myself, no one parties harder than a mom on a vacation from her kids.

†CPM = cost per "mille." "Mille" is the Latin word for thousand.

STEP 4: PRODUCT-MARKET FIT

Technocratic patriarchy limited access to this network for a majority of our sisters, but at least we got to pee in peace.

While there were few women, there were even fewer Black people at this conference. In fact, I saw exactly one other Black person, who was working a booth for a tech company. We locked eyes for a moment. He quickly looked down at his "tech uniform"—a black Patagonia fleece vest with his company's generic techy logo, bright blue polo shirt, and khaki pants—then looked back at me with an expression that said, "I wear FUBU and Karl Kani on the weekends."

However, I had just spent three days at the BlogHer business conference with thousands of women—and many women of color. I had a number of discussions with friends who were leading interesting startups focused on rethinking things like agricultural markets and diapers. Women founders, especially women of color founders, definitely existed, but we weren't present in the spaces where deals and investment flowed.

Thus, digitalundivided (DID) was born. I started DID in 2012 with a series of events called FOCUS100—with the goal to help one hundred Black and Latinx women get funding and support for their startups by 2020. The name "digitalundivided" was born out of the digital divide in the tech world, the difference between the availability and adoption of technologies in marginalized communities from rural to urban areas, from people of color (POC) to white communities, from high-resource to low-resource communities.

Today, the vision of DID as a business makes a ton of sense. Gathering Black and Latinx women building amazing communities into one space to ideate, incubate, and connect is a no-brainer opportunity for investors, right?

Yes . . . and no.

What I Did Right in Building the DID MVP

To sketch my first MVP, which was for a conference called FOCUS100, I used the resources I gathered from BlogHer and developed an initial pitch deck (we talk about how to create this in Step 6) that laid out the event. I spoke with Elisa, one of the founders of BlogHer, about the idea, showing her my initial pitch deck. She not only gave great feedback but gave me the BlogHer event operations manual (!!!) and $5,000 of seed money to get started.

> **Builder Trap: Going from Zero to Sixty in a Day**
>
> I know how hard it is to NOT bet your entire savings on your big idea, and I know this from previous experience. We Builders are told from birth by our families to always put our best foot forward. So the idea of putting a less than perfect idea out there is a tough pill to swallow. When I was building digitalundivided, I put over $30,000 of my own money into the conference. I basically went from pitch deck straight to big conference (Girl, no!), without pausing to see if there was a product-market fit. I had a product (the conference) and a market (companies that want to reach women of color), but at the time those two didn't match (more on that later).
>
> If I had done a much smaller conference for our first post-MVP product, maybe even just a small dinner that could have been sponsored by an up-and-coming tech company, I would have learned that at the time the market for my product was very small.

STEP 4: PRODUCT-MARKET FIT

People Like Visuals

Okay, so, maybe going from a concept to a large conference wasn't the best idea, but you know what was a great idea? That initial pitch deck. Not only did it help me land our first check, but it gave us a front-and-center seat to opportunities to grow our business.

Why? Because people LOVE visuals.

Most people are visual learners, so having a visual representation of what you're doing really helps many people to understand. Even though I had successfully built TBF and was "100 percent that bitch," a bitch still needed validation for her brand-new world-bending idea to bring the badass women of color to the front lines. That simple pitch deck allowed me to secure that first batch of funding so potential customers and partners could see what I was doing.*

> ### Tool: Create Your First MVP
>
> **Take a paper napkin, towel, scrap paper, etc.** Then do a schematic, drawing, or sketch of what your product will look like. It could be the actual product or a flowchart for a more service-based product (this is particularly good for software).
>
> Congratulations! You have just completed your first Minimal Viable Product in less than thirty seconds.
>
> As Builders, don't fall into the trap of not trusting the easy. Can I really get feedback on my idea from a napkin or simple website landing page?† Yes, you can.

---

*We review pitch decks in Step 6, but head online to geniusguild.co for examples of great ones.
†I'm obsessed with the TV show *The West Wing*, which is about the fictional presidency of Jed Bartlet. In episode nine of season three, Leo, his campaign manager, future chief of staff, and BFF,

I shared my hella basic MVP with a friend who was an executive at Ogilvy, who told me that the marketing giant had just opened an event space within their amazing new offices on the Hudson River in Midtown Manhattan. She offered the space to us for free (including food). Another friend worked with the big Silicon Valley venture capitalist firm Andreessen Horowitz (a16z), which was thinking through their diversity strategy. A16z invested $10,000.* We also had a connection with American Express from an old client of mine at TBF, and they became our major sponsor. I reached out to Darlene Gillard Jones, who I worked closely with on a number of successful projects at TBF and, later, BlogHer, to manage the logistics of the conference. Darlene, a core member of my personal advisory board, is incredible at managing challenging situations and people.†

The first conference was *revolutionary*. It might not seem like a big deal in the age of Kamala Harris, but back in the day in 2012 there were fewer than one hundred Black-women-led startups *total*. In the end our post-MVP product, even with its faults, started an incredible movement. And I am proud of that.

Building the MVP for Our Taco Truck

Let's use the food truck example from Step 3 as an example of how to build a quick MVP. We want a way to test whether or not there's interest in a taco truck. A quick way to do this is through a simple landing page, a basic one-page website that explains your business and collects contact information, like email addresses, that can be used to reach potential customers when it opens.

---

is trying to convince a reluctant Governor Bartlet that he should run for president. How does he convince him to run? He presents him with a napkin on which he has written "Bartlet for America."
*Ten thousand dollars doesn't seem like a lot in the context of the billions that a16z has under management, but VC firms rarely spend any money on initiative ideas that aren't directly related to a company in their portfolio.
†We call Darlene the "crazy whisperer" because she has had to manage some doozies during our time working together.

STEP 4: PRODUCT-MARKET FIT

Why are we starting with a simple web landing page instead of a tricked-out taco truck for our first MVP? Remember, the goal is to spend as little as possible on this initial MVP. While we *think* our community wants a taco truck, we don't *know* they want a taco truck. The only way for us to find out is to share a version of our product with potential customers. At this beginning phase, we spend as little money as possible until we have enough data (which we will get in the Measure phase) to bring us closer to knowing that our business is, in fact, a business.

Using an existing template of a WYSIWYG website builder company like Squarespace, I built our truck's MVP in less than fifteen minutes. I added a form to capture contact information for the taco lovers in our community (Measure), adding Google Analytics to learn additional details about the market like where visitors are located and how they accessed our page (mobile? desktop?).* It costs less than twenty-five dollars

Our Fifteen-Minute MVP

---

*It's super easy to add Google Analytics to your site within a website builder such as Wix or Squarespace. Just register your site in Google Analytics (https://analytics.google.com) and then head to your website builder to connect the accounts.

per month, which leaves me plenty of money to promote the business to the target market and get early feedback.

> ## Builder Trap: Spending Too Much Money on the First MVP
>
> Look, I know how tempting it is to think, "My idea is the best thing since wine popsicles; why don't I go all in?" or "My site looks like it was designed by a five-year-old hopped up on Halloween candy; let me just throw a lot of money at it so I can make my MVP great."
>
> It's easy to give in to the temptation of thinking that our MVPs can be made better by money. Yes, money can make your MVP better looking, but it still won't tell you if it's something people will actually buy. Remember, you're just trying to get enough information to get to the next B-M-L cycle.
>
> In 2018, I attended my very first Essence Music Festival, an annual event held during the summer in New Orleans, with three nights of the best music (Mary J. Blige! Prince! Mariah Carey!), networking (Oscar winner Halle Berry and I had a deep discussion about being Black women CEOs), and a sea of Black hair laid for days.*
>
> I was there for a panel hosted by the Case Foundation, which was started by billionaire entrepreneurs Steve and Jean Case, builders of the OG internet service provider America Online (AOL). The panel, which was sandwiched between a panel led by rapper/businessman Master P and a talk by Kandi Burruss-Tucker, a true polymath business-

---

*Hair that looks very nice.

STEP 4: PRODUCT-MARKET FIT

woman/singer-songwriter/Real Housewife of Atlanta,* was on African American entrepreneurship. It was a great discussion, to a mostly empty auditorium—hard to sell people on building companies when there's a food demonstration led by Boris Kodjoe right next door.

Afterward, an amazing founder, who we will call Mary, approached me. She had built an app that allowed salons to manage their bookings better. It was *very* similar to the previously mentioned Squire app. She shared her idea and a bit about her background with a lot of passion. Impressed with her idea, but knowing she was going to need a robust tech stack (the technologies used to run her app) to actually execute the idea, I asked her if she was an engineer or, if not, did she have tech co-founders. She paused and then answered no—she had withdrawn $35,000 from her 401(k) to work with outsourced developers in Ukraine to build a fully functional version of her idea.

Was that the right decision?

Let's take Mary's idea through the problem/elevator pitch exercise we did in Step 3 here to find out:

- **The problem I'm solving is** reducing the time salons spend managing appointments. (*Great.*)
- **The idea I'm building is** a mobile app to manage appointments. (*Awesome, it's tech enabled so it's highly scalable.*†)

---

*For *RHOA* fans, I had an amazing backstage conversation with Kandi's mom—Mama Joyce—where I tried to explain what a tech accelerator program was. Mama Joyce, who looked absolutely fabulous, gave me the standard reply given when a Black mom doesn't know what you're saying but wants to be encouraging: "Oh, that's nice." Now that I'm a Black momma, I find myself doing it to others ALL THE TIME.

†As stated before, not having a tech co-founder isn't as big of a problem as it was a few years ago.

- **This is a problem for** 700,000+ cosmetologists, barbers, and hairdressers in the United States. (*YASSS! A big market.*)
- **This problem** occurs several times a day. (*OMG, I'm sold.*)

Yes! All good so far.
So now here comes Mary's problem.

- **The customer currently solves this problem** by using Squire, StyleSeat, Vagaro, and a billion other apps. Many of these apps are incredibly well funded with solid engineering teams and a good amount of market recognition.

If Mary had brought me a sketch of the idea on a napkin or showed me the WYSIWYG landing page she created for $25, I would have told her about the other companies solving this same problem and possibly helped her save $35,000, plus the costly fees she incurred by withdrawing from her 401(k) account.

Another reason why you don't want to spend all your dough on the MVP is that you will leave little to no room to course correct or pivot. And if there's one guaranteed thing you will have to do when building your startup at least once (but more likely A LOT), it is to pivot. If Mary would have built an MVP using the 10 percent of her exit formula rule and then sought feedback from investors and people in the startup space, she would have had enough money and time to really figure out how she wanted to use her resources.*

---

*In Step 6: Getting the Bag: How to Get the $$$ You Need to Grow Your Company, we discuss in detail different ways to raise capital for your company.

Check Out These Under-$100 MVPs That Ended in a Major Win

Me & the Bees: Mikaila Ulmer became a beverage mogul at the age of ten years old, when she pitched her budding lemonade business, Me & the Bees, on the popular show *Shark Tank* and received $60,000 in investment from Daymond John. A year after starting a lemonade stand in her neighborhood, her drinks are sold in over fifteen hundred retailers around the country.

Zappos: Aspiring shoe tycoon Nick Swinmurn had a vision of selling shoes online, but he didn't have the shoes yet. His MVP was a website featuring a collection of pictures he surreptitiously shot at shoe stores around town. But through the simple passion of one low-fi sneakerhead and a few connections to the right people, the Amazon of shoes was born.

Measure: Get Feedback on Your MVP

You've completed the first leg of your very first Build-Measure-Learn cycle. We now have an MVP that took less than fifteen minutes to build and cost us less than twenty-five dollars per month. Next comes the hard part: getting feedback on your idea. This is where all the mental prep work we did in Step 1 comes in handy (told you it would be worth it). Yes, it's hard to be vulnerable and share your ideas with others. But it's equally hard to dig yourself out of financial debt for a business that no one wants.

Remember: Building a successful business isn't about what you want, but what customers want.

People Lie: How to Get Real Feedback

Now, let's talk a little bit about who to get feedback from. As entrepreneurs, we like to think our ideas are great. We love them and nurture them like children and can't wait until they graduate to make the big bucks. It's for that reason that it's hard for us to see when our ideas are real stinkers. And because most people don't relish crushing someone's idea, we often never receive the truth about the merits of our idea (or its lack of merits) until we've spent money and time building a bad product.

Tool: The Ugly Baby Test*

The Ugly Baby Test helps you to quickly find out whether or not there's interest in your idea. The test is simple:

1. Build a simple landing page, like we did for Terry's Taco Truck, using an online web-page builder.
2. Create a prompt that can accept email addresses.
3. Write a short (fewer than fifty words) description of your company/product. Make sure you clearly explain what you're doing.

---

*All babies are beautiful and should live without judgment. And for the record, my son is adorable.

STEP 4: PRODUCT-MARKET FIT

4. Head to Google Ads (google.com/adwords) and/or Facebook Ads and select three or so terms related to your business.

5. Set the option to maximize for clicks (not impressions). Impressions are how many people saw your ad and clicks tell you how many people were interested enough in what you're saying to them to take action.

6. Choose simple keywords that are linked to your product. For example, if you're selling custom teddy bears, choose "custom teddy bears," "custom stuffed animals," "custom toys," etc. as your main keywords.

7. Take note of how much it costs per click—the higher the click cost, the more competition there is for that keyword, and that could be an indication that there's a lot of interest in your field as well. Lower click cost could mean that either your idea is very new (less competition) or that there isn't much interest in your idea. How do you know which it is? Keep going.

8. Set a budget for a hundred dollars (NO MORE) and a timeline for one week.

9. Measure the click-through rate of your ad.

The average click-through rate for Facebook ads is 0.89 percent, so any rate that is 1 percent or higher is good and shows that there's some interest in what you're building. The average click-through rate for a Google ad is 2 percent, so anything above 2 percent is considered great.

It's important to get as much feedback as you can from people who aren't your friends or family, who are most likely to buy and use your product or service. Your dad willingly wore the bedazzled maroon tie your eleven-year-old self bought him for Father's Day. Your bestie assured you that "buzz bangs" were a thing after your hairdresser decided to "try something new." You need the truth and you need to get it from someone who didn't lovingly sit through your clarinet recital.

If we're Terry looking for feedback on his taco truck, we should head to the local food truck park because those are people who are current food truck customers and would most likely be our first customers. Before our town created the food truck park, we might have gone to an area that had a ton of restaurants on a busy night and approached customers who were waiting for a table.

Use the results of the Ugly Baby Test to prepare three to five short questions to ask potential customers in person. Try to keep them as open-ended as possible and stay away from yes and no questions. Starting with the words "what" and "how" is a great way to keep your questions open-ended:

- "How does this make you feel?"
- "How do you currently solve the problem?"
- "What are other companies doing to solve this problem?"

Avoid questions that start with "why," as that often comes off as defensive.*

Notice that I'm not telling you to ask "Do you like my idea?" Frankly, it doesn't matter, as most people will say yes to your face—whether they like it or not. Observe their body language as you explain your idea. Do they seem engaged or bored? Are they animated when talking about the problem or do they seem distant?

Record their feedback in a notebook or on a spreadsheet. It's important to not just record what they say but also look at their body language

---

*Think of the difference between "Why do you cook your own tacos?" versus "How do you cook your own tacos?" One is more accusatory and the other signals more a curiosity.

and listen to their tone of voice. What you're looking for is to see if your idea engages them. If they pause before answering you, for example, it means that the idea intrigues them and they're thinking about it. It doesn't mean that you have your *final* idea. But it does mean that the problem and your solution are intriguing enough for them to pause. And intriguing is good.

People like free stuff, so by spending as little on your MVP as possible, you have space in your budget to purchase giveaways to entice people to speak with you. For example, you can hand out fifteen five-dollar gift cards to the local coffee shop as a thank-you for those who took the time to share their feedback.

Focus on gathering as much information as possible. Ask food truck customers waiting for their orders questions about how often they visit the food truck park, the type of food they think is missing, and their feeling about tacos. Walk around the park and take note of the other trucks, the type of cuisine they serve, their prices, and the number of customers they have in an hour. Also note how customers are paying (cash app? credit card? cash?).

Record all this information (aka data) in your notes to review in the next and final leg of your B-M-L cycle—Learn.

Tool: Some Other Places to Get Feedback on Your Product/Company

PLACE	BOLDNESS RATING On a scale of 1–10 *how bold do you need to be to do this*
Social media groups Post a link to your idea and a description explicitly asking for feedback in popular social media groups that would be interested in your product. Popular forums like Reddit and social media platforms like Facebook have thousands of focused channels/groups with your future customers. **Tip:** Make sure to read the group rules so you don't violate any posting rules.	**1**
Offline interest groups Social groups are a great place to get feedback because your shared interest creates a level of familiarity with you, yet they're not your family—so they have a bit more space to be honest. Bring your MVP to your next church meeting, pickup basketball game, or knitting club. **Tip:** If you're prone to holding grudges, ask another group member if they would be willing to share the MVP for you and synthesize the data so the feedback isn't connected to a specific person.	**3**
Local meetups Check out local in-person or virtual meetups in your community centered around your company's product. **Tip:** You can find groups on sites like Meetup.com or Nextdoor.	**6**

STEP 4: PRODUCT-MARKET FIT

Conferences Conferences are great places to score feedback as attendees aren't just interested in the topic, but they're interested enough to pay to attend a gathering. **Tip:** Need help finding a conference for your market? Search "[your business category] + conference" in Google.	**8**
The mall You know those people who stop you on the street to ask your opinions on the plight of the rare golden phoenix? Yes, you can use the same tactic to garner opinions for your idea/company. Take a clipboard (or your phone) and head down to the local mall. Approach anyone you think might be interested in your product and politely ask their opinion. Yes, you will probably be ignored, but it is a great way to observe the body language of potential customers. **Tip:** Stand in front of a store that is popular with your target market.	**10**

What I Did Right and Not So Right in Getting Feedback for digitalundivided

To be perfectly honest, I did everything wrong when getting feedback for digitalundivided. The epidemiologist in me cringes while I write this, but the fact is, I don't think I measured anything other than the frequent flier miles that I got for traveling around the country.

Now, I'm not saying we didn't *get* feedback. We did, we just didn't *measure* it. I basically forgot (ignored?) everything I learned at Yale and didn't systematically collect and measure the feedback, let alone analyze that data and then use that analysis to make DID's product better. Remember what I said about the difference between a business and a hobby? Well, since I spent over $30k of my personal money to keep the company afloat, digitalundivided was a hobby.

Skipping the Measure leg of the cycle meant I skipped the Learn leg as well. If I had followed the cycle I set out in this step, I would have learned that while corporations, DID's target customer, were willing to invest some dollars to find Black *employees*, there wasn't much of an appetite at the time to invest money to find Black *innovators*. This mattered because in most companies the diversity, equity, and inclusion (DEI) budget is significantly smaller than the research and development or mergers and acquisitions budget.

While our community of Black and Latinx women did pay a conference fee, it wasn't enough to actually cover the cost to produce the conference. We did have some earlier supporters like American Express, but most of the initial checks were super small—$5,000 to $10,000. That wasn't enough to build a sustainable business model.

Here's what these sponsors knew that I didn't know: in 2014, it was virtually impossible to get a sizable check ($25,000 plus) written for sponsorship of a startup event focused on Black women entrepreneurs. One supporter at a major tech company told us that when she pitched her white male boss on sponsoring FOCUS100, he told her, point-blank, that Black women in tech wasn't a market they were trying to connect with. The $5,000 to $10,000 checks we were given was the amount of discretionary money that our supporters at top organizations like Google could write without having to go through layers and layers of approvals to get real money.

Even having support from celebrities wasn't enough to convince the corporate world of the value of the conference. Our very first FOCUS100 keynote speaker in 2012 was (then) Newark mayor Cory Booker, who had

STEP 4: PRODUCT-MARKET FIT

built a civic tech startup called Waywire. The following year, we had an actual pop star, MC Hammer, an early investor in companies like Facebook and Pinterest.

So FOCUS100 wasn't making any money. Being revolutionary didn't pay the bills. I often had to write checks from my bank account to cover our expenses. I remember one particularly challenging event in Detroit. It involved spending an entire day with Hammer, meeting with startup founders going through local Detroit incubator programs like Grand Circus and Pony Ride. Hammer had agreed to spend the entire day with us for $5,000, which was basically free. Right before I was to interview him in front of hundreds of people at Tobias's old high school, Cass Tech, his assistant Mike told us that the final $2,500 hadn't been cleared.

I was MORTIFIED. Hammer told us not to worry about it and was willing to still do the event. However, it wasn't acceptable to *me*—I needed to find $2,500 in the next thirty minutes at five P.M. on a Friday. Thank God we found a nearby Chase bank that stayed open until 5:30 P.M. While we sent Tobias to get the cash, I was on the phone moving the last bit of money from my basic savings account to the business checking.* In the end, we had a great event with all the local media stations and over three hundred people.

Because I was so wrapped up in putting out a fire, I didn't observe the obvious feedback the situation provided, which was that my target customer, corporations, didn't understand/want/see the opportunity. It didn't matter that our conference was one of the first media mogul Issa Rae ever spoke at (TWICE). Or that I interviewed actor Omar Epps and

---

*There's more to this story. In the middle of a Q&A with the community, there was a tornado warning, we lost power, and the generators didn't come on. Hammer, in true boss fashion, KEPT answering questions. In the dark. He then stayed and took pictures with EVERY attendee.

became friends with Hammer,* who became a big supporter of our work at digitalundivided. Corporations didn't see the opportunity and wouldn't see it until the murder of a Black man in my hometown of Minneapolis forced them to see it.

What to Do If the Feedback Is Bad

One of the challenges in receiving feedback is being open to the fact that your idea may not be great. It is no fun to hear that what is a beautiful "baby" to you is a gremlin to another person, but I've seen so many entrepreneurs fail because they were too afraid to receive feedback. They took a mediocre idea to market before it was ready because they just didn't want to hear it. The sad part is that their businesses could have been great, if they had only received the right feedback to help transform their original idea.

Feedback makes your business better. Negative feedback is just as important as positive feedback. Find out what you'll have to solve before you go to market, and you have a much higher chance of success. It's not easy. I'm still scared to face the criticism, and you probably will be too. But it's a *necessary* process—so strap on your mental fortitude, sit back, shut up, and listen.

I'm happy to say that *because* of my experience with digitalundivided, I am now relentlessly committed to getting AS MUCH FEEDBACK AS POSSIBLE. While building Genius Guild, my current company, I sought ruthless feedback as often and as early as possible. The earlier I hear the feedback, the quicker I can fix the problem and move forward.

---

*MC Hammer was born Stanley Burrell, but his legal name really is MC Hammer. Like on his driver's license. #blessed

Learn: Implementing the Feedback

So you've got a ton of great feedback. Now what? The next step is to take this feedback and use it to build a better version of your MVP. Your first task is to spend a bit of time diving deeper into the market around your idea.

Many books will tell you that researching whether or not your idea has a market, aka customers, is the first thing you should do. I suggest waiting until you get the initial feedback on your basic MVP. As a visionary, doing market research before you see the initial excitement your idea inspires can be very discouraging. For example, while digitalundivided fundamentally changed an entire industry, if I had done market research prior to putting together our first pitch deck (MVP), I probably wouldn't have started the organization at all, as there weren't (yet) customers for what we were building and we didn't have access to a VC sugar daddy (or momma) to invest in our vision. Spend this phase learning more about your market, your customer, and the opportunity.

> **Builder Trap: The Balancing Act—Community and Customer**
>
> When pinpointing your market, it is vital to strike a balance between your community and your customer. A customer is someone who buys your service/product. Community is those impacted by your product/service. Your customers are always a part of your community, but not all your community

> may be customers. For example, how many times have you hung outside of a coffee shop with a group of friends without buying a coffee? Instagram is full of companies with large social media followings but little to no revenue. Both customers and community are key stakeholders, meaning they are extremely important to your success. But to stay in business you have to make sure you are serving the needs of your customers first.

Don't get too distracted by appealing to the community. Just because you build it and your community loves it does not mean paying clients will come. As a Builder, be aware that you may need to go the extra mile in helping your customer understand the value of what you're selling and the value to the community you're selling to (especially if it is a community of color). Also be aware, as we learned building digitalundivided, that your target client may never understand the value. When building DID, I needed to spend a lot more time not just collecting feedback from potential partners but also learning more about their needs and what they valued. This would have provided clarity in what we were selling, how we needed to sell it, and how it solved a problem for our partners.

Congrats! You Completed the First Round of the Build-Measure-Learn Feedback Loop. Guess What? You Get To Do It Again! Yippee!

As a startup founder, you must constantly refine your product as you get additional feedback, especially once you go into the market and measure data from real customers. Analyzing this data and incorporating the learnings into your next Build is how you get closer and closer to product-market fit.

The work you do in going through the B-M-L loop will come in handy while working on the next part—the Business Model Canvas.

Mapping Your Business: The Business Model Canvas

The only thing I wish I had known when I started DID (but most definitely know now) is that a lot of the initial challenges with the digitalundivided business model could have been worked out by using the Business Model Canvas (BMC). The B-M-L loop is the process that gets you the information you need to build out your BMC. It would be nearly impossible to truly know your value proposition—what problem you're solving for your customers—without actually having them engage with your product/company. The BMC, developed by Swedish management theorist Alexander Osterwalder in 2005, is like a kinder, gentler version of the old-school twenty-five-page business plan. The Business Model Canvas helps you figure out how you are going to make money. It works via building-block questions to prepare you for the main aspects of a business model: Where is your money coming from? Where are your resources coming from? What is your pay structure? What are your relationships with your customers like? These questions then become the backbone of your business model.*

How to Build Your Business Model Canvas

>**Value proposition:** Your unique solution to your customer's problem. We've already completed this in the last step, so you are ahead of the game!
>
>**Key partners:** Who do you need for your business to be successful? This is where you list the key people you need on your side. It can be an individual (a great accountant) or a group of people (a web development team). List the types of partners you need (and why).
>
>**Key activities:** This is where you talk about what you need to do to fulfill your value proposition. These activities fall into three areas—creating and manufacturing an actual product (production), solving the problem you wrote in Step 3 (problem-solving), and building and maintaining

---

*This is a quick snapshot of the Business Model Canvas thought process. There are a number of BMC templates and resources, including the book by Osterwalder himself, that go a bit more in depth and provide additional guidance on the process.

the way you get your product to your customers and how they utilize it (platform).

Key resources: These are the important building blocks (inputs) that will let you build and grow your company. Think about all the inputs you need. A great team (human resources) is a very important resource. Access to investment and capital is another important resource.

Customer segments: These are the different types of customers you are trying to target. Try to group customers in categories. For example, if you were building a website for moms, you might group customers in terms of stage (new mom, school-age mom, moms with teens) or geography.

Customer relationships: Here you describe the type of relationship you will have with each of your customer segments. Let's take an idea for a new restaurant. Will you provide your service in person (like Applebee's)? Will your customer serve themselves indirectly (like in the IKEA cafeteria) or even via machines (like French fry vending machines in the Netherlands)?

Channels: Explain how you will communicate with your customers. Will you reach out to them via radio ads? Or maybe develop a robust Instagram outreach plan? The more specific you can be about the channel(s) you will use, the better. Instead of saying you will reach your customer via social media, say which specific social media channel you will use.

Cost structure: Think about all the costs associated with your startup. You don't have to list the actual costs, but you should list all the things that you have to spend money on for your business, like staffing costs, travel, etc.

Revenue stream: Here indicate how much money you will make and how you will make this money (aka your revenue stream). Will you sell subscriptions to your service (like Spotify) or will you start a marketplace where you connect sellers and buyers like Etsy?

Eight Popular Business Models for Startups

Choose one of these business models to help you figure out your revenue stream.

MODEL	DESCRIPTION	EXAMPLES
Marketplace	Charges a fee to facilitate transactions between buyers and sellers	Online marketplaces like Etsy, eBay, and Upwork
Subscription based	Just as it sounds, customers buy subscriptions to an ongoing service or product	Streaming services like Netflix and Hulu, meal prep box services like HelloFresh and Home Chef
On demand	Service is available anytime the customer requests and customers are charged after use	Ride-hailing apps like Uber and Lyft

STEP 4: PRODUCT-MARKET FIT

MODEL	DESCRIPTION	EXAMPLES
Disintermediation	Customers can only purchase the product directly from the company	Home shopping networks like QVC and travel goods companies like Away
Freemium	The basic service is free, but you want to get rid of the annoying ads? Unlock direct messaging? All those features that are just out of your grasp? You're gonna have to pay for that.	Online "radio" companies like Spotify and Pandora. Content services like YouTube and some of the U.S. network television stations' streaming apps. Online media companies that limit the number of "free" articles.
E-commerce	Sell a variety of products in an online store	Online superstores like Amazon and Jet.com
Ad-based model	Sell advertisement (including sponsored content)	Most online media sites, like *The New York Times*
Reverse auction	Buyers create the request and vendors/sellers bid to service it	Job boards like TaskRabbit and Thumbtack

At the beginning, resist the urge to try to develop your own business model—PICK ONE OF THESE. Why? Because it will make your life easier and reduce the risk to your bank account. These models are already proven to be able to create scalable businesses. You will have a ton of documentation on how these models have been implemented in other companies and you can learn from their wins as well as their failures. If you decide to seek funding, potential investors know and understand these models.

Don't be afraid if your model changes. It *will* change with feedback and as your product evolves. But do your best to be as detailed as possible in the beginning and you will be rewarded for your efforts.

Mayvenn: Example of a Builder Business Model in Action

African Americans spend approximately $2.5 billion on hair care products each year. I'm probably personally responsible for a good billion myself. Diishan Imira saw the absurd cost of extensions and weaves and wanted to find a way to save money for both customers and stylists and started Mayvenn, the global hair extension brand.

Imira had the smart idea to use a disintermediation business model to create a tech-enabled wholesale hair extension company. Armed with an ability to speak Mandarin, Imira set up a supply chain in China and bought wholesale hair extensions, which he then sold directly to shop owners at a wholesale rather than retail price. This not only empowered shop owners and benefited customers but was an excellent business strategy because Imira (and his investors!) got a cut of the profits. Soon venture bigwigs such as Ben Horowitz joined in to support the startup. Now Mayvenn has a valuation of over $100 million and a network of over fifty thousand stylists.

When Business Models Go Bad: What I Did Right (and Not So Right)

My company digitalundivided faced a big problem: we pitched partners on a product that in theory they wanted (Black and Latinx female entrepreneurs) but that in reality they didn't see the business imperative for. We didn't have the seed investment to focus on continuing to develop our product while we waited for the corporate market to mature to the point of seeing the value of our community. We were too early. In 2012, when I started digitalundivided, there was little to no discussion about Black women in startups. Had this been 2021, investors might have seen the value in what we were doing. But this was not the case in 2012.

In 2014, we had to officially shut down the FOCUS100 conference. I had a choice: I could continue to spend a ton of my personal savings, eating into the gains from selling my company, or we could turn digitalundivided into a different type of business—a not-for-profit corporation. I knew from discussions with friends who were in the economic development space that philanthropy was willing to bet on what we were building. I chose the latter.

That said, even in the nonprofit space we had our work cut out for us. The narrative for so long in nonprofits had been to focus on the perceived deficiencies in the Black community instead of bringing to light what we had to offer. In other words, we had to fight to convince people to invest in the potential and brilliance of Black and Latinx women entrepreneurs.

So I announced to our community on October 13, 2014, that we were closing the FOCUS100 conference, letting the room full of amazing Black women know that this was the last year we were holding it. Our last few moments were spent in a cathartic discussion, basically a good old church revival, about the challenges of building a startup as a woman of color.

After I made my final tearful speech, actress Anna Deavere Smith came up to me, looked me in the eye, and said, "You have a gift." These encouraging words at this difficult time led me to a moment of clarity: FOCUS100, and possibly digitalundivided, might have been over, but I wanted—no, I *needed*—to leave something good behind. Something that other women of color could build on.

ProjectDiane and the Importance of Data

I try to live by the simple principle that you should always leave something better than how you found it. It is a lesson I learned from the amazing life of my father, who had close to a thousand people at his funeral. What we were trying to do with the FOCUS100 conference in 2014 was too early. But I wanted to make sure by the time the next incredible woman came along to try to build this—and there would be a next time—they would have a foundation to build on. The ridiculous challenges we and every other Black woman faced building a startup needed to be documented.

I knew I wanted a way to really illustrate the years of abuse, because there's really no other word for what women founders, especially Black women founders, have to endure. Sexual advances masked as pitch meetings. Spinning your wheels in fundraising hell because you never receive *real* feedback on your startup.

The inspiration for how I would document this came from my husband, Tobias. I was sharing with him my frustrations and how I was trying to figure out the best way to capture the very real challenges faced by women in startups. I was so angry that there was no data on women-led startups, let alone minority-women-led startups. Crunchbase didn't even have data on the gender of founders in their database, yet alone the data on race. So yeah, we all knew that the startup world was everything but diverse, but no one had actually thought to count.

My husband listened patiently as I bitched about the lack of data on anyone with a tan in the tech and startup spaces. He waited until I took a much-needed breath and said, "Didn't you graduate, with *honors*, from Yale University with a degree in research? Why can't *you* do this count?"

Sometimes as women, we look for answers in everything and everyone *but* ourselves. We have the solutions to our problems (and other people's problems too). It was such a simple, obvious answer that I completely didn't see—until a man suggested it. Every feminist bone in my body aches just sharing this story with you.

So I started the first ProjectDiane, a comprehensive biennial research project that gathers data on Black women startups, with zero dollars in funding and seven outsourced Ukrainian data collectors on Upwork, while building a company that didn't have a sustainable business model. That was okay, because I could do it. Yes, the startup world did not see the value in Black-women-led startups, but I did. We spent HOURS combing all sixty-thousand-plus entries in Crunchbase. I got friends to give us access to PitchBook. The women-led database site Mattermark was the only startup data site to give us access for free. We literally searched those sites for anyone who had anything that looked like a dark tan. I asked all my friends in venture capital to send me the names of all the Black-women-led startups they knew. Each one sent me the same three names. It was very sad.

That's how I made the venture capital world pay attention to Black women. The results were shocking—but in hindsight not really that surprising. In 2015, when I started the project, there were only eighty-four startups led by Black women. Only eleven of those had raised more than $1 million in venture capital funding. At the time there was only one Black female general partner of a venture fund, Kesha Cash, out of more than a thousand VCs.*

One.

I named ProjectDiane after Diane Nash. She was the most important civil rights activist you've never heard of. In her teenage years, she joined

---

*A venture capital fund is really a company (sometimes two to three companies). The general partner is the manager of the fund, like a CEO, and is responsible for the fund's investment thesis and making investments in startups. It's a BIG deal to be a general partner in a fund.

and eventually became head of SNCC (the Student Nonviolent Coordinating Committee). There is a video of her confronting the mayor of Nashville in 1964. Just imagine a young Black girl telling off a fifty-something white man for endorsing segregated food counters. Yeah, she was a badass. I chose to honor her and carry on the legacy of all the amazing things Black women have done.

Still, would these stats be enough to make a difference? I was saying to a friend of mine and her partner that I wasn't sure if the tech world would support this research project because it would mean they would need to actually acknowledge they needed to change. My friend's partner piped up, "You know, we have a CTO at my company who would be interested in this. I've got five thousand dollars in my budget I can give you, and I'm going to help you promote it."

From there, I wrote an article on Medium and sent it out to friends and relevant sources. We also did a Kickstarter, setting a low bar of $25,000, and we ended up raising $50,000 in forty-eight hours. People were emailing me to say, "I've always wanted to help you do what you're doing, thank you for giving me an opportunity to help." It showed us that what we were doing was important. There was a community out there, now proudly wearing our sparkly Kickstarter T-shirt swag.* I wasn't the only one who thought Black female entrepreneurs mattered.

ProjectDiane 2016 sparked a nationwide dialogue about inclusive entrepreneurship and innovation. Since the release of this project (and in no small part because of #ProjectDiane), the number of innovative start-ups founded by Black women has more than doubled and the amount raised by Black women founders increased 500 percent, from $50 million in 2016 to $250 million in 2017.

---

*More on how to build a successful crowdfunding campaign in Step 6. Let's just say people LOVED a good sparkly tee.

ProjectDiane was supposed to be my swan song to digitalundivided. But the data actually showed exactly why we hadn't found product-market fit with our initial business model (it was due to some nasty little factors outside my control, like systemic sexism and racism). We used the data from ProjectDiane to develop the BIG Incubator Program (BIG), which guides high-potential Black and Latina women founders of tech-enabled businesses through a twenty-six-week program based on the Lean Startup Methodology (LSM) model to empower Black and Latina entrepreneurs and strengthen our community.

Don't get so caught up in what you are doing that you don't create space to learn how to do it. Of the many lessons (sooo many) I learned from building digitalundivided, perhaps the biggest is putting my faith in the process (in this case Build-Measure-Learn) in order to get to my end goal, which was to increase the number of Black (and Latinx) women entrepreneurs in the startup space. After millions of dollars raised and thousands of people helped, I did that.

You GOT this.

Keep company with good people and good people you will imitate.*

Proverb

*The original quote, featured in *God's Little Instruction Book for Students*, reads "good men" instead of "good people." But it's the twenty-first century, not the 1800s, so I changed it. #shedidthat

STEP 5

Squad Goals: How to Build an Amazing Team

There is a direct correlation between *market* fit and *team* fit. When you have a good fit with your team, the path to finding and maintaining product-market fit is much easier. When you are in alignment with your team, you're able to develop versions of your product quicker, respond to external challenges fast, and stand in your leadership confidently.

In business, it's essential that you surround yourself with good people, the *right* people. This isn't to say that if you choose not to work with someone, they are not a good person. It may simply mean that they are not a *good fit* for your company. Managing people is a skill, and it takes a great deal of work to get good at it. But once you do and can spend less time managing your team, the more time you have to dedicate to other areas of your business, like acquiring customers.

Squad Goals: How to Build Your Team

So how do you find "good" people?

First, Be a Good Leader

In order to build and lead a great team, you have to be the kind of person who *people want to build with*.

What does that look like? It looks like centering your humanity (yep, those core values again) by remembering at the end of the day that we all want to live a creative life that we control. Entrepreneurship is just the tool we use to do it.

I've always been a leader, since building my first business in the fourth grade.* But it took a great deal of personal growth for me to become a good leader.

Tool: Five Tips for Being a Great Leader

1. Stay healthy. Eat regularly. Get good sleep. Stay hydrated. Keep moisturized. Exercise. Believe me, all of these things matter. If it's three P.M. and you haven't eaten since eight P.M. the previous night, do you think you're going to be able to make the best decisions for you and your company? Hell, no.

---

*I cornered the Minneapolis elementary school friendship bracelet business. At one point I was bringing in fifty dollars a week, which gave me the ability to make loans to my older brother (at competitive interest rates, of course).

Have a snack (or two). I swim five days a week at the local gym, especially during super-stressful times.

Staying healthy means taking care of your mental health too. Let me tell you from experience: being a mother, being a wife, and being a CEO simultaneously is no picnic. Sometimes *you* need help, and that's okay.

2. Abide by your own core values. Remember the core values we defined in Step 1? You are going to use these A LOT. Tape them on your wall. Set them up as a pop-up on your computer. Live by these values and do not second-guess them (or yourself).

3. Be open to learning. As a CEO, I think it's critical that you ABL: ALWAYS BE LEARNING. I realized after several years of being a CEO that when I didn't have the time to myself to think and process and learn from the world around me, I wasn't making the best decisions. Now, I block time on my calendar each week for me to read and absorb information to make me a better person and a better leader. I believe that this solo learning time is essential for everyone. Take at least an hour a week to give yourself permission to reject all calls and focus on new ways to learn and better your business without outside interference.

4. Take joy in your work so you are a joy to be around. Sometimes being a good leader means you are just enjoyable to be around. As a leader, you have to find that JOY in your job so the people around you find joy in their jobs.

At Genius Guild, we have a robust internal Slack community where we talk business but also about other things. We have a whole channel dedicated to that 2021 meme of Bernie Sanders at the presidential inauguration. We have long discussions about hair weaves (#bestedgesinvc). We create Spotify playlists that feature everything from trap music to Gregorian chants.

> **5. Know when to walk away.** Sometimes being a good leader is recognizing when something isn't working. Sometimes businesses fail. Sometimes even relationships fail. Sometimes it's not your fault. Sometimes it is. And sometimes your company is thriving but your personal life is crumbling (and vice versa). My advice? KNOW YOUR NUMBER. Know what your breaking point is. Identify the point at which you're willing to walk away in order to preserve your sanity, or your dignity, or your marriage, or your relationship with your family.

Every time I've failed as a leader, it was because I didn't follow these five tips. Staying a good leader is a continuous process, even more so in this post-pandemic world where team members may be dealing with a variety of anxieties and stressors. It's impossible to truly be there for others if you aren't there for yourself. Martyrs are selfless people who give their lives to a cause (or in this case a company). They are also dead.

So there's no need to be a martyr for your business. There's no value in assuming that role for you or for your team. Just as you are a reflection of the people you surround yourself with, they are a reflection of you. Your business is a reflection of you. That goodness starts *with you*.

Your First Employees

In the beginning your first employees will fall into these three groups:

- Friends and family
- Co-founders
- Employees and consultants

Friends and Family

Friends and family are often the very first helpers, when we're at the earliest stage of building our companies, especially before we have actual revenue. Our familial networks are important tools for Builders. You can get the labor you need to get the first versions of your product out the door or much-needed staffing while you're building up your customer base at a relatively low cost. However, like any resource, it must be managed diligently or else you run the risk of losing it.

When my family started the dry-cleaning business, I didn't understand the connection between market fit and team fit. I was twenty-four years old and it was my first foray into entrepreneurship. I didn't even think about the importance of either of those elements separately, let alone together, in the creation of a business. All I wanted to do was just build. And not understanding the deep partnership between market fit and team fit almost cost me my relationship with my family.

But while the impact on our personal and financial lives was painful, I did learn some very real, very hard lessons about building a business, especially building a business with loved ones. As per the quote at the beginning of this section, my family are good people. In fact, they're great people. I am also a good person. But we weren't a good fit for one another in business.

My advice to Builders is to try to work with your familial networks to build the MVP until you've actually figured out your product and the market you're trying to fit it to. The reason why I give this advice is that your familial networks have a vested interest in your success outside a paycheck, therefore giving you some latitude. Being late on a check for your brother is very different from being late on a check for an employee or consultant. But at some point, you'll probably need to move on from building with your family.

Working with (and Managing) Family

So how do you manage your first *human* resource (aka friends and family) when you are just starting your company? Family often equals a sense of security and love and belonging. It also comes with a lot of complications that we *don't* think about.

It's simply human nature: *Your role in your family is the role you will play in the business.*

It doesn't matter if you have an MBA from Harvard and were employee number six at Google. To your family, you're Li'l Sis/Mommy/Cousin/Pookie/Chica. Family members have a hard time seeing one another in roles other than those they play within the family. In my family and our dry-cleaning business, I was the prodigal daughter. I had been away at college and graduate school for over six years, coming home for holidays but never really staying for longer than a few weeks. My family didn't know me anymore and I really didn't know them.

I didn't realize how coming back with my East Coast bravado and giving orders to the people who gave orders to me for my first eighteen years would affect them. Imagine your baby girl questioning your leadership decisions or your little sister giving you career advice. What I needed was to step back and let them get to know me and vice versa. But of course I didn't. Like I said, I was twenty-four.

One more thing to consider: *You love your family, but do you LIKE and RESPECT your family?*

There is an enormous difference between seeing your family on holidays and working with them every day within the stressful context of building a business. You have to like to spend long, extended periods of time together AND you have to respect them. If the previous sentence made you pause, DO NOT start a business with them.

STEP 5: SQUAD GOALS

You might find out that while you enjoy spending time with them, you might not enjoy working with them. I'm a bit OCD when it comes to exceeding expectations, and I thought my family understood this and recognized that it was how I got through a very competitive school like Yale. But I am sure it appeared, at times, as if I was a bit of a know-it-all. I suspect if my brother was to be completely honest, he would not have included me on his list of favorite people at that time. Again, in my case, a lot of the issues stemmed from not really knowing one another and our capabilities. I think if my brother could have seen the process, the work, and the sweat it took for me to be me, he would have had a different perspective on my work ethic and why I was so driven.

> ### Builder Trap: Not Getting Buy-In from Your Support Network
>
> One of the biggest mistakes I've seen startup founders make is not getting buy-in on your new business from your core support group. Remember that personal board of directors from Step 2? Yeah, you are going to need their help as you develop your company. Whether the core support group is a partner or a roommate, it's important to make sure that those loved ones feel confident that you can run a company AND be there for them.
>
> I'm not saying it will be easy, but you've got to sell your loved ones on your business and the values behind it first. Because, again, startups are mentally and physically exhausting. You need help from *everyone*. Think of the people in your home as your behind-the-scenes team. I recommend a good heart-to-heart with those loved ones, asking those tough questions and outlining the big issues, from

> how you're going to manage finances to who's going to do chores.
>
> The very first person who I had to sell on Genius Guild was my husband. At that point, he'd been through so many startups with me, from my crash-and-burn dry-cleaning biz to the success of The Budget Fashionista to the emotional roller coaster that was digitalundivided. He knew what he was getting into, but laying it all on the table beforehand made us more prepared for what was to come.

Founders and Co-Founders

One of the biggest questions I receive from startups is whether or not they should bring on another founder or co-founder (yes, these are different things). The answer: it depends. First, realize that there's a difference between someone you started your company with (founder) and someone who was the first employee once you had your MVP (co-founder).

TITLE	DESCRIPTION	HOW THEY ARE PAID
Founder	Someone you literally started your business with from square one. You came up with it together on a random Tuesday afternoon over two glasses of pinot gris.	Paid more in equity than salary

STEP 5: SQUAD GOALS

TITLE	DESCRIPTION	HOW THEY ARE PAID
Co-founders	Someone you or another founder brought into the business at the beginning but wasn't involved in the ideation phase. Think of them as your first hire and an important part in building out your product or service.	Paid more in salary than equity

Pros of Bringing on a Founder/Co-founder

- **You might have an easier time getting funding.** There was a time when it was virtually impossible to get venture funds if you didn't have more than one founder. It is not as difficult now, but you still might have an easier time getting funding with another founder or co-founder on your team.
- **They can help fill in the gaps.** Do you have the skills to run your company? Do you know how to make your product? Do you know how to sell your product? Maybe you're the ideas person and you need someone to come in and make it happen. A co-founder might be the right choice for you.
- **They take some of the weight off your shoulders.** I often suggest that if you have other things going on in your life, like if you're a mom or a primary caregiver, then it's a good idea to get a co-founder to help share the load.

Cons of Bringing on a Founder/Co-founder

- **You have to like your founder/co-founder, like, a lot.** You have to ask yourself, "Could I spend a significant amount of time with this person? Could I be in constant contact with this person for the rest of the life of the company?" No? Then this is not the person you want to run your business with you.
- **Founder/co-founder conflict is no joke.** In fact, 65 percent of startups fail because of it. As in any relationship, poor communication is often the root of conflict between founders. Establishing your personal and company core values early on, and communicating them to each other, is so important to building a successful relationship with your co-founder.
- **You have to negotiate everyone's different tolerance for risk.** The concept of risk is vastly different for everyone, and having a clear discussion with potential partners about how they view risk is crucial before jumping into a business together. When my family started our company, my brother had a wife, a mortgage, a toddler, and a baby on the way. I was a newlywed with few expenses other than student loans. Our abilities to take on risk were very different, yet a majority of the day-to-day stress was placed on my brother as the COO—on top of the responsibilities of being the "man" of the family and having to handle his own grief over our father's passing. As a founder, I should have understood how much riskier the business was for him than for me.

Pointers on Building a Successful Founder/Co-founder Relationship

Let's say you start your business with a founder or co-founder. Great!

First things first: Communicate clearly and consistently with one another. Make sure each person involved understands why you're all starting this business and confirm that you're all on the same page. Though it might sound counterintuitive, not everyone goes into business to make money, and differences on this front can cause BIG problems. For example, my mother saw our business as a way to continue and grow my father's legacy, while I saw it as a way to make some serious money (which also furthered my father's legacy). Those are two very different visions. I think if we had sat down and clearly laid out each of our visions, things might have turned out differently.

> **Exercise:** Have each partner take out a sheet of paper and create two columns, *Responsibilities* and *Importance*. In the Responsibilities column, write down each of your responsibilities (e.g., children, mortgage, geriatric pets), and in the Importance column, write down how important each item is to you. For example, for some, the stability of owning a home is very important, while others value the flexibility of a rental. Owning a home presents a higher financial risk because it's much easier to break a lease than a mortgage. Learning what each of you value will help to mitigate risk and maximize your sense of safety, support, and potential for growth within the company.

After you've done this exercise, it's time to outline what you will be contributing to the company. And this is very important: *get it in writing*.

When there are complications with your founders and/or co-founders, having a document to refer to can be very, very helpful. For example, if one founder says, "Well, I'll do all the work if you give me all the money" but then you find out they're playing video games for sixteen hours a day, you know that they're not holding up their end of the bargain. You then can go back to your original contract to make your case for why you are hesitant to invest more time and money in the business.

When outlining responsibilities between co-founders and founders, specificity is your friend. For example: "I'm going to work forty hours a week on x, y, z projects, and then co-founder Jenny is going to put in a million dollars and we're going to split the profit fifty-fifty. Our ownership is tied to these two things." It's important to define the relationship at the beginning and get everyone to sign off on it. Google "co-founder breakups" and you will get pages and pages of horror stories, often due to one person carrying a majority of the workload. The worst part of these stories is that unless there was a vesting clause (we will discuss this in the next step) the person doing most of the work may not be able to get equity back from the other party who's been sitting on their butt the whole time.

Make sure to go back to the question posed at the beginning of this step: Can I spend eighteen hours straight with this person, six days a week? If the answer is no, you might want to reevaluate the partnership.

You will be spending a lot of time together. So. Much. Time.

A test is to schedule a road trip with the possible partner. You learn a great deal about someone once you have to travel together. A (minimum) three-day road trip is a great way to gauge whether or not you could spend extended time together in a situation that can get super stressful.

At the beginning of digitalundivided, Darlene and I took a road trip where we visited local tech incubators around the country. One of our stops was in Charlotte, North Carolina. Before we could leave there was a massive snowstorm. The snow was so bad that Walmart ran out of food and we had to fight (literally) for the last head of lettuce and jar of olive tapenade.* We were stuck for three days in a Holiday Inn with three boxes of instant soup we scored from the hotel vending machine, a single head of lettuce, the tapenade, and each other. Since we were the only people at the hotel, we spent a great deal of time talking, sharing, and swimming in the hotel pool. Darlene and I learned that not only could we build a business together, but that we worked well together in pretty challenging situations. We finally were able to get on one of the first flights to New York after an Entitled decided to give up his seat because the Westchester airport was too inconvenient for him.†

Consultants and First Employees

There will come a time—for some sooner rather than later—when you will have to bring in outside employees or consultants to help you continue to build and scale your company. One of the hardest decisions as the founder of a new company is to know when to bring in outside help. Some people would say to bring on people as soon as you have a bit of revenue and/or raise your first pre–seed round of outside funding. Others say wait, especially for salaried employees, until you know that you have a recurring stream of revenue.

---

*Even under stress, we maintained our bougie credentials.
†Dude insisted that he "must go to JFK or LaGuardia Airports only." Depending on where you're going in New York, both airports can range from twenty minutes to one or more hours from your destination. The Westchester County Airport (HPN), a charming smaller airport, is about forty-five minutes from New York City.

Defining Your Company's Values

Remember in Step 2, when you defined your personal core values? You're now going to do the same for your company. First and foremost, before you bring anyone from outside your circle in on your business, you have to know what values drive it. Building a team is building a community. And communities, especially startups, are built on a foundation of shared values.

As a Builder, I believe that this values-first approach is especially critical. Many of us are striving for economic stability. There are so many factors in our day-to-day lives that make us feel unstable. We might have left our home country to make a better life in the United States. The systemic racism in America means our civil rights feel tenuous. We might have language barriers that hinder our access to resources.

Business, especially startups, is inherently unstable. Joining a startup is even riskier for those in marginalized communities. As a founder, you can't offer the same type of stability that a traditional corporate job can offer. Jobs change. Funding runs out. Ideas don't achieve product-market fit. So what makes an employee want to sign on?

Your Company's Core Values Provide a Sense of Stability to Staff at a Startup

Building our core values was the first thing I did when starting Genius Guild. These values are the foundation that supports everything we do—from how we invest to hiring team members. It's through these beliefs that we communicate a shared value system. As the CEO of a startup, it would be impossible for me to provide stability around job descriptions or even business models. But where we *can* provide stability is around our eight core values. The implementation of these values may expand, but the core eight won't change. So instead of a new employee basing their social contract with Genius Guild on a job—which, again, will change in a startup—their relationship with us is built on the core values.

I developed our core values in partnership with executive strategist Valeska Toro, who also led our core values work at digitalundivided. Creating the eight principles that constitute Genius Guild's core values was the first actionable thing I did when I started to build the company. What we were creating was going to be complicated, and I wanted to make sure that we clearly communicated our values to potential investors, partners, and team members.

Genius Guild Core Values

CORE VALUE	DESCRIPTION	CORE VALUE IN ACTION
1. Be human	Trust the good in others.	Trust your team. Celebrate their wins and empathize with their losses. In challenging times, refrain from judging or blaming, and focus on learning and evolving together. In practice: • We make assumptions every day. Be clear on what your assumptions are. • If you identify an assumption, seek clarification. Ask the questions that need to be answered. • If you make a judgment, assess how past experiences or confirmation bias may be impacting your perception.

CORE VALUE	DESCRIPTION	CORE VALUE IN ACTION
2. Be abundant	Believe in a world where everyone can win—including you.	The world is inherently abundant. Everyone can win. At Genius Guild, we strive to make this a central truth. In practice: • Strive to make decisions and take actions that benefit all parties involved. • If your decision or action disadvantages a person or group, rethink the approach. • Identify if "scarcity" is impacting your approach or decision. Determine if it is a fact or a feeling.
3. Be brilliant	Practice your genius every day.	In practice: • Identify what your genius is—What do you love to do? What are you great at? What are your core strengths? • Bring your genius to work every day. Your perspective and skill set matter. Don't be afraid to express the first and put the second to good use. • Learn what other people's genius is. Empower them to contribute in a powerful way.
4. Be brave	Take the risk.	It is possible to take a risk and win. Great outcomes require great courage. By being brave, we make significant shifts. In practice: • Make decisions and take actions with the end goal in mind. • If a risk is required to achieve an outcome, communicate it and assess the impact. • Get clear on what you're afraid of and how it's affecting your decision. Step outside your comfort zone.

CORE VALUE	DESCRIPTION	CORE VALUE IN ACTION
5. Be mindful	Practice active listening.	Active listening allows us to fully understand the problem we're solving and make thoughtful, informed decisions. In practice: - Be present in conversations and meetings. Eliminate distractions and listen to what is being said. - In making decisions, consider every viewpoint and understand the broader context. - Ask powerful questions. There is always something to learn.
6. Be agile	Move, learn, and evolve quickly with confidence.	Evolution is a natural part of who we are. The quicker we move and the more we learn, the sooner we can achieve our highest performance. In practice: - Identify what is necessary to achieve the outcome. Distinguish and remove wasted energy or work. - Just start. - Make time to evaluate learnings and pivot on a bimonthly basis.
7. Be open	Speak your truth and the truth of others. Honor your word.	Trust and honesty go hand in hand. Be honest about your thoughts and listen to the thoughts of others. Once an agreement is reached, honor your word. In practice: - Be concise and direct. Share what is *really* going on. - If you succeed, own the success. If you make a mistake, own it and learn from it. - You don't have to agree with another person's point of view—but you do have to understand it and work together. - Engage in thoughtful disagreement. Create a win-win.

CORE VALUE	DESCRIPTION	CORE VALUE IN ACTION
8. Be committed	Commit to your growth and the growth of others.	To grow, we must practice self-awareness. Know your strengths and work on your weaknesses. Learn with your team. In practice: • Identify your strengths and weaknesses. Make a plan for improvement and growth. • Be open to others' feedback. They want to see you succeed. • Create a structure to give and receive feedback from key people on a consistent basis. • Wherever possible, provide feedback to others in the moment so they can work on it right away.

At Genius Guild, we are human beings (GG core value #1), which means there will be times when we may not live up to our values. Human beings are fallible. And that is okay. The goal of the core values isn't to create a restrictive set of rules that need to be followed religiously on a daily basis. Instead, the core values are guideposts. If one team member isn't living up to these values, then it's the responsibility of all the others to help them get back into alignment with our goals.

The core values are also an invaluable decision-making tool for our team. They provide direction on who to partner with (and who NOT to partner with). It's baked into the due diligence process for Genius Guild's venture fund—the Greenhouse Fund.

After my experience with my previous businesses, I made setting my core values my first priority when I start a new enterprise. I do this before

I even think about hiring other people. Then, after I set my core values, I take this values-first approach to the next level by hiring people based on these values.

As business owners, we often find it challenging to hang our hats on our values when hiring instead of, say, putting a person's skills or job title as our number-one ask. Different Builders and different companies need employees with different skill sets and strengths. That, combined with lots of legal requirements that also vary for everyone, means I can't give you one-size-fits-all advice about how to interview and what competencies to make sure you have. But the one thing that is absolutely universal is to make sure you share values.

But here's the reality: As a startup, the job of anyone you hire in the beginning probably will change at some point. What won't change is the values. This is why, instead of centering our team on the jobs we need done or even on our business model, we center it on a set of shared values. As you'll see later in this chapter, all of the hiring mistakes that I've made were because the shared values weren't there.

> **Builder Trap: Pushing Aside Core Values**
>
> It's easy to push aside what your core values are, particularly in the stressful moments in the infancy of a business. So I highly recommend writing them down and putting them somewhere you can see them every day. I have my core values in a note on my phone.

So how does Genius Guild realize these core values? Here's an example. One of the values at Genius Guild outlined above is "Be abundant." Abundance mindset focuses on possibility and scarcity focuses on limitations. At Genius Guild we see the world as full of infinite potential. We believe the universe wants you to win. Money, success, and impact are not limited, they are plentiful and free-flowing.

Another example: I experienced a major shift in priorities, like most people, during the pandemic. My family became even more of a priority for me and I set a goal for myself to make sure I always center them. As a result, we decided to move from Atlanta (where we had no family within a twelve-hour drive) to Chicago (where 99 percent of our family was within a three-to-six-hour drive). At the same time, I was finishing up this very book, raising money for the Greenhouse Fund, and managing a team. In the midst of all of this, I forgot the one thing I was supposed to always center: taking care of my five-year-old son. Kids have a way of forcing you to focus on what really matters. While everything else needed me, he *really* needed me. So I had to be vulnerable and trust that the team (core values #1, Be human; #7, Be open; and #8, Be committed) I built would give me the grace I needed to help him (and myself) through the move.

To be honest, 99 percent of the GG team really stepped up to help me through this difficult time. My assistant (now our chief of staff) quickly assumed that leadership role. A member of the ops team quickly took ownership of the completion of our websites. Our VC in residence stepped in to handle fund operations.

Unfortunately, one staff member had a challenge with it. At the time I was hurt by her lack of understanding. *However*, in hindsight, it was a great stress test for the company. Particularly challenging times offer you the opportunity to see if the culture you've built is strong enough to weather the storms to come. Not only did my team give me the space to give extra love to my son, they gave me the space to see who on the team was aligned with our core values.

It's incredibly important to create a company culture where you as the CEO have the space to be human as well. Showing a bit of vulnerability can bring your team closer, helping some discover leadership skills, like our chief of staff, that they didn't know they had. It can also cause tension, especially for those who don't work well in spaces where their leaders show their fallibility, their humanity. Many of us have been taught to "never let them see you sweat" and that "mistakes are weakness." So when they see you, as the leader, make a mistake, it challenges their worldview about leaders. This doesn't mean that the person is a bad employee or person. It just means they're not a good fit for your company. And that's okay.

What Should I Look for in New Hires?

As CEO, it is your job after setting your values to find and recruit those people who are a good fit for your company. This is, of course, easier said than done. Look for potential employees who have these three beliefs:

1. **Believe in your core values.** As we discussed earlier, it's so important to be on the same page about values from the beginning. If your core value is honesty, ask potential employees outright a question like "When was a time that being honest cost you something important?"
2. **Believe in your product/service.** You need the people you work with to believe in what you're selling. How can your team sell your product if they don't believe in it?
3. **Believe in you.** You cannot build a business by yourself. You need people who believe in you and respect you and like you as a leader.

The three beliefs are incredibly important because as a Builder, you are going to have enough challenges with people outside your company. You don't want to face those challenges internally as well.

I once had a male contract employee in charge of writing all the content for a website for my venture studio. The business's core demographic was the Black community. The content guy, who wasn't Black, was, unbeknownst to us, giving direction to the design team to use clichéd, outdated slogans on the site like "Bet on Black." We found out and I told him, "Phrases like that are very clichéd in our community." He then proceeded to inform me, a Black woman and his client, that I was very clearly wrong. He was promptly relieved of his duties.

The contractor felt that he knew more about my business and my community than I did. I had to remind him that I had been Black my ENTIRE life. No one knows more about your business than you. You have to have people who value you and your expertise. Your goal as CEO shouldn't be to convince somebody that you deserve to lead. They should already know that. And if they don't, then you need to let them go. Quickly.

Hiring a team member is a two-way relationship. It's not just about a good fit for you, but also a good fit for the potential employee as well. My advice is, if you can, before bringing anyone onto the team officially, test the relationship first by hiring them as a consultant with a mutually agreed upon time limit (usually no more than three months) paid at the monthly equivalent of the job at the full-time rate.* This is a great way to see if they are a match for you and if you're a match for them. If it isn't a match on either end, it's an easy out to part ways at the end of the three months.

---

*Make sure to check with your state's labor department to confirm you can do this. We do give most of our benefits, like flex time and paid time off, to contractors, except for health insurance, as insurance companies require staff to be employees in order to receive this benefit.

Also, many talented people want the flexibility of being a consultant, rather than being an employee. That's especially true after the pandemic. As a potential employer my advice is to consider the best relationship for your business. Ask yourself, "Is it important (and is it legally required) to have this staff member as an employee or is it more important to have the person and the skills they bring? Is this person handling sensitive information that requires liability or data storage insurance coverage, which is often limited to employees? What type of safeguards do I have if things don't work out?"*

In order to get talent to stay you will need to incentivize them. The primary way to do this at the early stage of your company is through stock options. It's important to note that these options are vested over a set of years (usually at a set vesting rate), which incentivizes people to stay in order to realize their options. This can also work the other way, with staff members who would have voluntarily opted to leave instead staying on until their options are fully vested.

The question of vesting, how much equity to give and on what schedule, is very tricky, and there's really no right answer. In my experience, I've rarely seen early staff (not co-founder status) receive more than 1 percent in equity vested over a period of three to five years. This means that the employee doesn't get their full 1 percent equity until they've been with the company for at least that long. This is to incentivize employees to stay at the company and rewards them for taking a risk on a new company (versus going to work for the local corporate giant).

---

*Since each state has its own rules and the law is constantly evolving, it's a good idea to speak with a local attorney familiar with employment law in your state.

> ### Builder Trap: Pay Attention to Employment Law
>
> Make sure you pay attention to employment laws, as they vary from state to state, especially for independent contractors. What one state considers an independent contractor, others consider an employee. Make sure to have a contract setting the terms for the relationship from a legal standpoint. If the relationship isn't working, then you have a timeline in print for when the relationship will end without necessitating a major confrontation when you terminate the relationship. If it is working, then it's easy to set up another contract or develop an employment contract, if necessary.

A note about business consultants: Consultants should only be hired for discrete specific projects with specific goals and a specific end date. DO NOT hire consultants before you've actually built the business. When building the dry cleaners, the vultures saw us and our naïveté and grief coming from a mile away. They also saw the family drama and found a way to manipulate it to their (very pricey) benefit. We hired expensive "consultants" who somehow convinced my grieving mom that spending $30,000 for two days with a former IKEA CEO at his home in North Carolina was the same as sending my brother to get his MBA (trust me, it wasn't; if he'd gotten the MBA, he would have had something to take with him regardless of what happened to the business).

In my experience, you usually know pretty quickly who is going to work and who isn't going to work. I cannot emphasize this enough: trust your instincts. A great fit makes your work easier, so you can focus on building. We work with an amazing HR consultant who has helped me create HR and operations processes for my last two companies. She is incredibly competent and such a joy to work with on a daily basis.

STEP 5: SQUAD GOALS

These team members understand their role in the company and are secure in that role, which allows them to work without conflict. As a founder of a high-growth startup, your goal should always be to reduce the amount of unnecessary conflict in your daily work so you can focus on building and scaling the company. The saying "Hire slowly, fire quickly" is extremely important, especially in the beginning stages of your company. You don't have the time for assholes.

I've experienced the results of NOT trusting your instincts. At a previous business, I worked with an employee who was downright antagonistic to me from the beginning. On the first day in the office, in their FIRST meeting with me, they told me, "Well, maybe I made a bad decision. I shouldn't have come to work here." WHO SAYS THAT ON THEIR FIRST DAY? We haven't even met, yet they had decided that it wasn't going to work. Now, I should have said bye right then, but the Minnesota people pleaser in me was trying to make it work. I was in the middle of transitioning out of the organization, so I had relaxed my standards and just decided to let it go.

It. Did. Not. Get. Better.

I could never win with them, which in hindsight shouldn't have been a surprise because they literally told me at the beginning that I was in a losing position. I was in a constant battle with them, about everything, to the point that it became a distraction in the organization. When I did leave, I received immense support from the rest of the staff, who were excited for my next move. EXCEPT FOR THIS PERSON. Trust. Your. Instincts.

Who You Need to Hire

There are four archetypes that you need to have on your startup team: the Doer, the Lieutenant, the Strategist, and the Economist. There can be multiple people filling these roles or just one person per role or one person for two roles, but strive to have each of these archetypes on your startup team.

The Doer

Doers are the team players who do whatever is needed to get shit done. When you're starting a business, it's all hands on deck. Sometimes, you need people who are just going to do something without questioning every little thing and who you can trust to actually do the thing. These are the people that if you say, "We need a red sign," they will find you a red sign without a thirty-minute Lincoln-Douglas debate about why the sign should be red or passing the job on to someone else.

Doers often get a bad rep as yes-people who just rubber-stamp whatever you say without question. Yes, you don't want an entire team full of people who rubber-stamp everything. HOWEVER, you need people who will fill whatever role you need them to fill. For example, we had an employee who was hired to help us build partnerships who, in the nascent stages of our company, did some much-needed pinch-hitting in marketing because she had that background and we didn't have a full-time marketing person yet. You want those jacks- and jills-of-all-trades in the chaos of the early days.

Keep in mind that in the beginning, as CEO, you will need to be the doer as well. When we fired the content guy who knew more about the Black experience than his Black boss, I had to jump in and write our web content until we hired our head of brand and marketing. Why? Because after years of building, developing, and selling content properties, I had the background to be able to pick up the slack. I spent the first warm weekend of the year inside writing the web copy so our site could be ready for our launch. So I embraced the doer in me. I Got. It. Done. If you're not willing to grind as a CEO, you can't expect others to want to grind as well.

> **Builder Trap: Doing the Most**
>
> Yes, you will need to be able to grind as a CEO. However, you need to know when to grind and when to trust the grinding to others. I admit this is a challenge for me, even after building multiple companies with robust staff. I find asking yourself the simple question "Can someone else do this?" prior to going all in on a task particularly helpful. Asking myself these five words has saved me a bunch of time and helped me to build trust with my team.

The Lieutenant

Lieutenants are leaders who can translate your vision, make decisions, and provide directions to others based on this vision. When business starts ramping up, you do not want to be stuck micromanaging every employee. Part of building a good team is finding people who not only get the vision but also own the vision. This will allow you to focus your energies on making the important strategic decisions that are crucial to being a successful Builder.

As CEO, you want to reduce the number of decisions that you, personally, have to make so you can focus only on the most important decisions. For example, one of the most prominent jobs at the White House is that of chief of staff (COS). The COS is the right-hand person to the president and handles all the day-to-day running of the office, like hiring staff, managing basic meetings, and even making many decisions, so the president can focus their time on the high-level decisions.* Delegate or automate the easy decisions so you have the space to make the hard ones.

In most companies, the chief operating officer (COO) or director of operations often serves the role of the Lieutenant. Their focus is translating your vision into operational steps that others can follow. These ops superstars serve as partners to strategists on the team but have a laser focus on the analytical rather than the theoretical aspects of the goal.

The Strategist

These are the big-picture folks. They are the ones who can think two, three, four, five steps ahead. They are constantly asking, "What's next?"

There's a good chance that you as a CEO are a strategic thinker. If you're not, it's important to cultivate strategic skills by spending time doing a bit of free thinking. As I've said before, free thinking is giving yourself unstructured time to explore your industry, rather than doing tactical work on your startup. This is key. In the fast-moving, social-media-driven world we live in, there's been a devaluation of giving yourself the space and time to think and explore where those thoughts lead you. Block out time each week, as I do, to read books and articles about

---

*President Barack Obama not only delegated management of his office to his COS, but he famously went a step further and only wore blue or grey suits to reduce the number of decisions he had to make in a day. This freed up his mental space so he could make those super-important presidential decisions.

your industry. If you're Terry trying to build Terry's Taco Truck, you might listen to a podcast about food truck culture and then write down some thoughts about the industry.

In areas outside your areas of expertise, you want to hire people who can be strategists. Note: A high price, as illustrated above, doesn't mean that the consultant is the best strategist. You want to look for people who've actually built and implemented a strategy for your category of business.* For example, if you're trying to roll out your product and marketing isn't your area, then it's important to hire someone who not only understands how to write a tweet, but the strategy behind the tweet.

The Economist

Make sure you have someone on your team who understands the economics of the business and how money moves in your industry. Starting a business can be expensive, and often you lose money at the outset, so you need someone who sees a path to profit. This might be you as the CEO or it could be your COO. This person's role is to say, "Okay, we can make this happen. It's going to take six months and we're going to need to sell this much on these channels, and then we'll start turning a profit."

My advice is to be really honest with yourself. Look at your finances. Look at your history. Are you good with managing money? If the answer is "No" or a half-hearted "Maybe?" then bring on someone to assist.

While you can and many times should hire someone who has a solid understanding of the economics of the business, you as a CEO MUST

---

*I always start with LinkedIn to find those with the skill set I'm looking for and reach out directly. I then schedule follow-up calls where I ask how they've implemented the skills. I also ask to speak with someone they've worked with before and ask them specific questions about the skill set.

have a basic understanding of your business—what generates revenue, what the liabilities are, what your costs are, what your areas of growth are, and how much it will cost for you to get there. You cannot outsource this essential knowledge. Understanding these fundamentals makes the difference between whether or not you receive outside investment.

> ## Builder Trap:
> ## Not Understanding the Full Cost of Hiring
>
> If there's one mistake that I see emerging entrepreneurs make over and over again, it is not understanding the TRUE cost of an employee.* The hourly rate or salary of the employee is just one cost of having them. If you live in the United States, you will have to pay federal, state, and sometimes city taxes. You also have to factor in costs like payroll taxes (Federal Insurance Contributions Act, or FICA) that are up to 8 percent of the salary, unemployment insurance, workers comp insurance, and sometimes even a commuter tax. This doesn't even include health care and other benefits.
>
> If your business is located in a country outside the United States, make sure to understand the local and governmental laws around taxation, insurance, and things like national pension schemes. Hiring a local lawyer or solicitor with solid experience with national employment law will help keep you out of trouble.
>
> My advice is to always add an additional 20 to 25 percent on top of what you're already paying an employee to esti-

---

*We're focusing on employees as traditionally defined by the U.S. Department of Labor. Check with your state and/or accountant, but usually consultants are considered independent contractors, meaning they are almost like mini companies. As a result, you most likely wouldn't pay payroll taxes. Again, check with your accountant and/or attorney.

> mate their true cost. Let's say you have an employee making $50,000 per year; their true cost to your company is $60,000 to $62,500.

A Lawyer, Accountant, and Executive Coach Walk into a Bar: Subject Matter Experts

Employees aren't the only hires that count when it comes to starting a business. I recommend considering some additional hires: a lawyer, an accountant, and an executive coach.

Why a lawyer? Well, for legal issues. Most of us don't know the intricacies of the law, especially if we're a newer CEO. My advice is to find the most competent lawyer you can who fits into your budget. You want a lawyer who has experience working with businesses like yours. If you're raising outside investment, like venture capital, you will need a lawyer who has experience with common legal instruments like SAFE agreements and convertible notes.* When I started Genius Guild, I met with every major law firm in the startup space. Each proceeded to whitemansplain to me how what I was doing wasn't going to work—before really learning what we were even building. One dude even asked me if I was aware of the organization that *I founded* and was *the CEO of* for eight years. I found my current lawyer after chatting with a friend in the space about my challenge finding culturally competent lawyers.

---

*We discuss the wonderful world of SAFEs and convertible notes in Step 6.

> **Tool: Registering Your Company**
>
> You (probably) don't need a lawyer to set up your company. My family hired super-expensive corporate lawyers before we even had a business. This was because of our own naïveté and, to be honest, laziness. *Again, you should have one on tap to consult with on specific legal issues,* but you may not need them to file the registration paperwork with your local and state government entities in order to get started. You can do it yourself online or use a registered agent service like CT Corporation to help you file and keep up with the legal requirements.

Why an accountant? The IRS always gets paid. Ask any reality TV star. A good accountant will make sure you stay on top of taxes, especially sales tax, identify areas for tax savings, and provide general financial guidance.* As a business owner, especially when you have employees and significant revenues ($50,000 or more a year), you can't have your play cousin do your taxes.†

Why an executive coach? As Builders, we are met with a slew of cultural and socioeconomic challenges that can impede our ability to grow our businesses. For example, many of us come from families that have challenging relationships with money, and that can manifest itself in negative ways as we build our companies. Some of us have fears around the use of technology. An executive coach can help you work through

---

*Most startups now use online payroll services like Gusto and QuickBooks to help process and manage payroll, thus reducing the need for outside help to handle this aspect of your business.

†Unless your play cousin is an accountant, then work that hookup.

some of the challenges faced as you grow your business and your role as a leader. I hired an executive coach to help me work through the building of my company to the launch. He was extremely helpful in helping me stay focused on the launch and managing the day-to-day challenges of leading a dynamic company.

So what makes a great executive coach? Valeska Toro, Genius Guild's in-house executive coach and co-founder of the coaching service Uncommonly, shared the following characteristics of a great executive coach with me.

- **They are credible.** You want to make sure anyone you partner with has invested in themselves and possesses the proper skill set to support you in your transformation. The coach should have successfully graduated from a coach training program that is accredited by the International Coaching Federation.
- **They are objective.** A coach is different from a mentor or expert in that they are not hired to give you advice. Rather, the coach partners with you to help you define what you want, what is getting in the way, and what actions to take to move forward.
- **They believe in your greatness now.** An experienced coach knows you are fully capable of taking on your goals and creating what you want. They will refrain from changing or fixing you (as there is nothing to fix) while supporting you in expediting your growth.

So You Got a Team. Now What?

I've hired a TON of people in my career and the number-one lesson I've learned is that hiring is just the tip of the iceberg. The real work is in managing your team for success, and you can't manage a group of people toward success if no one knows what constitutes it. In order to do that you need a solid goal framework that defines and measures your shared goals.

Tool: The Power of Agile

The word "agile" is used a lot in the startup world. It's a project management process borrowed from software development that enables teams to set and accomplish goals and collaborate quickly and efficiently. It's through this constant collaboration that you are able to quickly process new information and make swift changes. Pretty much all tech companies use some version of the Agile methodology. Examples of non-Agile companies are old-school retail companies like Sears and Kmart, which weren't able to pivot quickly when it was apparent that the internet was going to disrupt the industry.

We use elements of Agile at Genius Guild. We hold daily fifteen-minute meetings (called standups) to just check in with one another and be able to provide any feedback or support needed. We also use project management software like Asana and communication tools like Slack to help

STEP 5: SQUAD GOALS

> facilitate the Agile process. These tools help keep us on track with ongoing tasks and provide internal messaging tools to keep our team in regular and easy-to-access communication both on the one-on-one and group level.

At Genius Guild, we use the Objectives and Key Results (OKRs) framework. First introduced by Andrew Grove of Intel in his 1983 book, *High Output Management*, an Intel employee turned venture capitalist named John Doerr brought this idea to a little (at the time) startup named Google. Here's what Google co-founder Larry Page had to say about it:

> OKRs have helped lead us to 10× growth, many times over. They've helped make our crazily bold mission of "organizing the world's information" perhaps even achievable. They've kept me and the rest of the company on time and on track when it mattered the most.

The OKR framework isn't just used by tech giants like Google, but also social enterprises like ONE, the HIV/AIDS awareness organization. OKRs are critical thinking frameworks where you set immovable objectives for your company and then set metrics—key results—for your progress toward your objectives. While objectives can be more abstract, such as "Increase awareness on social media," key results should always be easy-to-measure and quantifiable, such as "Increase organic Instagram likes by 20 percent." I recommend setting three to five solid objectives per quarter and two to five key results that will measure the headway you make toward each objective. Different team members can be working on different key results at any given time, but everyone should be working at all times to meet the ultimate objectives.

Example: Real Life OKR We Used at Genius Guild

			OWNER	MANAGER	DUE DATE	COMPLETION DATE			
OBJECTIVE: ESTABLISH THE GENIUS GUILD BRAND AS ONE OF THE TOP THOUGHT LEADERS IN THE STARTUP ECOSYSTEM									
						Q1	Q2	Q3	Q4
Key result #1	GG established as a brand with a fully realized brand strategy								
	Action	Develop strong brand strategy with clear OKRs							
	Action	Develop fully realized brand bible including logos, colors, graphics, icons, etc.							
	Action	Complete design of GG collateral (pitch deck, Zoom screen, etc.)							
	Action	Complete GG website design							

The beauty of OKRs is that they act as a guidepost for your goals as a company while allowing for flexibility in your means of achieving those goals. Your ultimate objective will never change, but how you get there, and the results you hope to achieve along the way, might change. With OKRs, you can tell your team members, "Okay, here's our ultimate objective. If this action doesn't serve our ultimate objective, then don't do it. Simple as that."

From there, it's an easy process of negotiation with key results. You might set as a Year 1 objective a 300 percent increase in social media following during the summer and set as a key result a big advertisement push on Twitter during the second quarter. Second quarter comes and goes, and you find that customers aren't responding via Twitter but are responding via Instagram. So adjust the key result to focus on Instagram. You keep the objective (300 percent increase in social media follows) the same but adjust the key results to match realistic expectations.

Key results shouldn't be the way you measure your individual employees' performance. It should be the way you measure your company's performance. This is a companywide effort toward progress, and the success or failure shouldn't fall on the shoulders of any one employee. This is, at its core, a wholly collaborative process.*

Remember, your goal as CEO is to minimize the number of decisions that you have to make. The way to do that is through trusting your employees. I recommend doing regular one-on-one individual check-ins with your staff at least once a quarter and meeting with your team on the regular. At Genius Guild, as I mentioned, we have daily fifteen-minute check-ins. During these check-ins, we ask questions like "What are your wins?" "What are your losses?" "What do you need help with?"

A daily check-in might seem like micromanaging, but in fact it is the opposite: they make your team *more* efficient. When we started doing these check-ins, we found that people were doing extra work that other people were also doing, so we were actually able to alleviate some of everyone's workload.

These meetings are short. So many companies make a fifteen-minute meeting into an hour-and-a-half-long rehash of everything they've been talking about for the last month. I recommend that meetings last *only* fifteen minutes. In fact, I recommend using a timer. The longer a meeting goes, the less efficient it becomes. It's one of those without-fail inverse

---

*Pick up John Doerr's EXCELLENT book *Measure What Matters* to continue to build your foundation for developing solid OKRs.

relationships, especially when you're talking over Zoom. The fifteen-minute mark is when someone inevitably whips out their phone under the desk to check their FB messages.

> ### Builder Trap: Getting Too Comfortable in a Post-COVID World
>
> Obviously, we have entered an age when geographic barriers no longer define the parameters of our businesses and our work. Especially with the digital innovation that arose during lockdown, online communication and working from home with people all over the world has become the norm.
>
> But be aware that communicating digitally is not the same as communicating in person. I recommend that, if you can get your company together at least once a year, it will go a long way toward establishing a clear sense of camaraderie and purpose. In times when you can't communicate face-to-face, I recommend using Zoom for difficult conversations. It is easier to communicate your intentions when you can see the other person's face.*
>
> Not only do you have to be very clear and direct in your intentions digitally, but you also have to set firm boundaries, otherwise it is far too easy to blur the lines between work life and home life. Too many people fall into the habit where the workday never . . . quite . . . ends when working from home. And it sucks. Set boundaries.

---

*Conversely, there's some research that points to the opposite being true. Author and cognitive psychologist Therese Huston believes that phones are better than Zoom for having tough conversations because while our facial expressions lie, our voices do not. I've experienced the exact opposite.

How to Fire

We've talked about how to hire, who to hire, and how to manage and grow the people you hire. Now let's talk about the flip side of that coin: firing.

Here's the thing: firing is a part of doing business. You can't keep people on your team who don't align with your company values and who consistently don't meet the goals and expectations of their work. I'll be so bold as to say that many of the major mistakes I've made in business were because I didn't fire someone quickly enough. I should stipulate here that your very first action when you start feeling dissatisfied with an employee's performance shouldn't be to fire someone, but to check in. "Here are the results we wanted and it's apparent that it's a challenge for you to achieve these results. Is there something else going on that is impacting your performance?" And it may well be that they are simply not equipped to meet the challenges you need them to. Or it may be that you have unrealistic requirements. Either way, opening this door allows them the space to tell their side of the story and, if it isn't something that has a fix, then you can let go guilt-free.

> **Tool: Finding Your True Calling**
>
> A strategy that has always worked well for me has been to ask the employee, "What is it that you *want* to do?" I often find that people who are struggling either have an answer that is in conflict with what they are doing or they don't have an answer at all. When someone's ultimate goal does not align with what they are doing, they are not incentivized to

> take steps to better what they are doing. And when someone doesn't have a clear objective, they don't have the means to reach that objective.

The Process of Firing

So how *do* you fire someone?

There is no easy way to fire someone. It sucks. No normal human being gets pleasure from firing someone. No one wants to have those tough conversations, but the difficult part is that in order to run a business, you have to have those tough conversations. It comes with the gig.

How do I do it?

First and foremost, I meditate. I find that it is so important to center myself in my humanity *before* I have a conversation with the employee I have to let go. By centering my own humanity, I'm able to see the humanity in other people. I ask myself, "How do I do this in the most humane, caring way possible?" The goal is to be in a compassionate frame of mind when I start these difficult conversations. That compassionate frame of mind helps me to root myself in the knowledge that everyone is a student of life. And we all want to be A+ students.

We are all here to grow and change and, sometimes, letting someone go is the best way to help a person find the place where they can be an A student. Many times in these situations no one is at fault. It simply is not the right fit. Yes, maybe that person isn't attaining the results you need. Or maybe you just have a feeling that something isn't working. Focus on where you want to go and where you need your company to go. If this person is not aiding in that journey, then they are simply the wrong match.

Once you've set your mindset, it's time to have the actual conversation. Going back to one of our core values, be honest. How do you do that and keep the no-fault mindset? You acknowledge that there is a *misalignment*, not fault.

There are also a lot of practical considerations to consider when you fire someone, and this is why writing down the offboarding process, the steps that need to be done to remove access to accounts, process last payroll, etc. for the employee, is so important. Depending on the nature of their departure, voluntary versus being fired, you might need to develop a severance package.*

Now, here's a sticky issue: How do you fire your friends and/or family members? Unfortunately, there's no easy way to do this, as you can't (and shouldn't) control their reaction.† But you followed the advice earlier in this chapter and set intentions and ground rules in writing, so you should be okay. The best way is to be very honest and direct with the person. Let them know how much you appreciate them and their work and how you don't want the job to get in the middle of your relationship—which is very important to you.

---

*According to Investopedia, a severance package is a bundle of pay and benefits offered to an employee upon being laid off from a company. In order to receive this package, the employee has to sign an agreement (called a severance agreement), which often includes language that prevents the former employee from disparaging the employer.
†This is the reason why many entrepreneurs, if they have the ability to do so, refuse to hire friends and/or family members.

Your Team Is Set. Now Secure the Bag(s).

As a Builder, assembling a solid team is crucial to your success as a startup founder and extremely important to your ability to raise funds to scale your company to the next level. The first proof that a potential investor has that you can sell your product is your ability to sell your first team members to join the company. However, most investors will want to know how you are incentivizing this team to stay on for the long term. I always ask this question of potential investments as a way to assess their thoughts on team building.* This wasn't always the case. Prior to 2012 or so, if you were an Entitled you could raise $1 million based on a drawing on a napkin. Unless you have a track record of startup success, those days are long gone. Often to raise that first bit of money to "seed" your company, you need some sort of MVP *and* a solid founding team to get to the next level. We talk about how to do this in our next and final step.

You GOT this...

---

*Think back to that discussion we had about equity and stock options.

Cash rules everything around me (C.R.E.A.M.)

Method Man, rapper and chronic (literally and figuratively) lover

STEP 6

Getting the Bag: How to Get the $$$ You Need to Grow Your Company

You've faced your fear (Step 1). Your personal core values are clear (Step 2). Your idea solves a problem and people are eager to pay you for your solution (Step 3), and you've fearlessly built a solid MVP (Step 4). You have a great founding team (Step 5) and you're ready to scale.

Now all you need is money . . . or do you?

One of the reasons I sold The Budget Fashionista was because I scaled the company as far as I could on revenue alone. In order to take it to the next level, I needed additional capital, preferably not from my personal banking account or utilizing my personal credit. In the startup world that can come from two main places: either from private equity (selling the entire company to an investment firm, which then runs the company while you become an employee) or from venture capital (selling a piece of the company while retaining majority ownership). Neither option was appealing to me. Though I was offered several million dollars in venture funding, I ultimately decided to sell the company instead. The investment from the venture firm would have required me to run the company, but I was ready to move on. The money, while nice, would have cost me my sanity, which is priceless.

Most early-stage entrepreneurs rely on three primary sources of startup capital: (1) personal and family savings, (2) bank loans, and (3) credit cards. Personal savings and/or support from your family is the most popular method (63.9 percent) used by new founders. Next is bank loans (17.9 percent) and then personal credit cards (10.3 percent). All of these sources are what are called "non-equity-based" funding, which means that these funding sources don't usually take any ownership (equity) in your company. Traditional crowdfunding is also an example of non-equity-based funding.

A distant fourth option, investment from angel and venture investors and equity crowdfunding, was a rarity for Builders until the global venture capital world was shaken awake by the murder of George Floyd. From 2018 to 2019, Black and Latinx women, who are more than 20 percent of the U.S. population, received only 0.64 percent of venture funding. Prior to 2018, only thirty-four Black women had raised more than $1 million in outside venture funding. In Europe, only 1.3 percent of venture funding went to ethnic minority startups and 1.1 percent to all women-led startups. It's hard out there for sisters and brothers in the land of VC.

However, pursuing the wrong type of money can be disastrous. Waiting to pursue outside funding allows you to keep control of your business and its direction until you're certain you've found the right people who will help you take your business where you want it to go for a reasonable price. So it's imperative for Builders to understand the world of startup funding. Venture capital or angel investment may seem like it's a great idea because the financial risk is assumed by the investors. HOWEVER, taking on this type of investment means you are taking on a partner/boss. With a loan or personal funding, you get to keep 100 percent of the equity (ownership) in your company. HOWEVER, you assume all the financial risk. That means if the company fails, you are personally responsible.

So what's the right type of investment for you? In this, our last step, I'll walk you through when to take funding, the types of funding, how to attract investors, and how to not dig yourself into a deep pit of financial despair by establishing your end game from the get-go.

When (and When Not to) Take Money

You've got a killer idea. It's tempting right from the start to want to go ALL IN and invest as much as possible so you can launch your business into the stratosphere!

Slow your roll, friend.

There's a reason why funding is the *last* step. Building a business as a Builder is *hard*. Building a business takes time. It's in your best interest to take your time clarifying your business, your company and personal values, and understanding your business model before raising any outside capital because all of these things impact the type—and amount—of capital you should raise.

When it comes to taking outside money, my personal rule is that you should aim to only take equity-based financing in order to scale your company and/or product. In other words, *take money to make money*. And I don't mean in an abstract "this-will-make-me-more-money-someday-if-it-works" kind of way. I mean in the way that you can see a direct A to B path of how this money can be a catalyst to generate more money in the not-too-distant future. The reason I say this is so you, as the CEO, have clarity and confidence in what you're building.

Let's go back to Terry's Taco Truck. You just completed your website, you have some great feedback, and you've learned that people really like the idea as evidenced by the number of emails you've collected via your MVP. To move to the next step, you're going to need to buy a food-service truck in order to cook and serve the food. The role that this truck has in getting your company from point A to point B is pretty clear, which makes it a great item to seek outside financing for.

When you consider pursuing outside investors, focus on centering one of these two objectives:

1. To exploit a rare opportunity (e.g., taking advantage of the ability to purchase equipment/product/another startup that grows the company's core business)
2. To scale your company after establishing product-market fit (e.g., your product sells out and you need to produce more, and you have a long waiting list for your product)

I do *not* recommend taking the investment to build your MVP. Wait until you've gone through a few B-M-L cycles. In the nascent stages of building a business, I recommend you use your own money (or free money like grants) as much as possible. As a Builder, I'd recommend only asking for outside money once you've established product-market fit (and, if you're a Builder, you will have to prove you have product-market fit more than Entitleds). The reason why is to reduce your personal liability* and for you to maintain as much ownership of your company as possible.

As an active investor, I invest in what I know: health and science, beauty and fashion, online communities, and companies that disrupt the

---

*The worst thing is to have to dig into your personal savings to pay back loans on a failed business.

way money flows in Black communities. As a founder, make sure any investor you bring on to your company has at the very least a basic understanding of the field your company operates in, which will mean you won't have to explain every little decision you make. I find myself really drawn to other founders with a strong science or tech background, especially Black women scientists. Of course, I've invested in founders who didn't have a science background. But, as a Black scientist, I know how other Black scientists think. Even if I might not fully get the field their specific company operates in, I have a clear understanding of them as a founder.

Not all money costs the same. Some money is very expensive.

Whatever you take away from this step, I urge you to take that away. POC Builders, particularly those of us who don't have a lot of money or grew up without a lot of money, may not have much experience with large sums of money. More importantly, we don't know that it's okay to say no to money. And it's important to say no to money when the price isn't right.

I once had a corporate partner that offered to give me millions of dollars for my company in order to be a passthrough* to a separate entity. I mean, it was A LOT OF MONEY. But I was leading a nonprofit. Taking money with the condition that we would pass it through to a for-profit entity was unethical. So I turned down the offer. But here's the thing: if I hadn't thought through the costs (to my personal morals, to the soul of the organization), I might have taken it. It was real $$$. However, I wouldn't have been happy with myself, so I turned it down. Needless to say the corporate partner wasn't happy (and neither was my business partner at the time).

In 2021, *Forbes* interviewed me about Genius Guild. I talked about how we were fortunate enough to be inundated with offers, good offers,

---

*An intermediary used to facilitate a transaction between two different entities.

from investors for the company. So many, in fact, that we had the luxury of saying no to some of those opportunities. I'll say here what I said in the interview because I believe it bears repeating: "Being a Black woman (or any person of color) and being able to say, 'I don't need your money' is a pretty powerful thing."

You do have a choice in your funding. Owning that choice enables you to hold on to your power as a Builder entrepreneur.

The Questions You Should Ask Yourself BEFORE Taking Investment

That said, in order to scale your business and get the right talent on board, you *are* going to need some money. So how do you know if you're ready for investment? Ask yourself these four tough questions:

1. Who Do You Want to Be in the World?

What is important to you? Who do you want other people to think you are? What are the core values both for you as a person and for your business as a whole?

The work you did on your personal and business core values (Steps 2 and 5) become super important. Yes, this seems a bit existential when thinking about money, but I believe that you have to know these answers *before* you ask for investment. Knowing will allow you to say yes to the right funding and no to the wrong funding. And that's no with a period, not no with a question mark.

For example, because I knew that the corporate offer for millions of dollars wasn't in line with my core values, it actually made my decision to say no fairly simple (but not necessarily easy). You see, when you're building a company, knowing who you are, what you care about, and what is meaningful to you and the company helps you to stand firm in all areas of decision-making—especially when it comes to funding.

2. Why Do You Want the Money?

As an investor, founders often pitch me. My first question is always, "Why do you need capital?" I can't tell you how many times the founders do not know the answer to this question. Knowing the why behind capital is as important as the how.

I once had a founder tell me that she wanted investment so her husband could leave his job. My thoughts: "This is such a red flag." For the record, I am not against spouse/partner teams at all. Maybe your partner *is* a talented software app engineer and might be the right person for the job, but *leading* with "I want you to give me money so I can hire my husband to work for the business" makes it clear that you are looking for money to give your husband a job.

Think back to our discussion in Step 3 about focusing on solving the problems for customers. Think of your potential investor as a customer; what we care about is how an investment is going to solve a problem for us (getting significant returns to our investors/partners). As an investor, I want to know that you will be using the money to grow and scale your *business*, and if said husband/partner is a person who can help you do that, then by all means, hire them. But that shouldn't be the central reason for raising investment.

Let's say the founder's husband was a software engineer. They could have framed their answer as "I need to scale and grow my business by hiring a full-time software app engineer." If your husband is the right fit for your company, as an investor I have no problem with you hiring them, especially if they produce results.

3. How Will You Spend the Money to Fuel and Scale Your Business?

Make sure you can articulate how you would use the money to get your company to the next step. Investors aren't doing you a favor by investing in your company, you are giving up a part of your company in exchange for capital to grow it.

I once had a brilliant entrepreneur pitch me for investment in her beauty tech company. She had a bomb team and a solid idea that she could actually execute. She was raising $1 million, a very reasonable amount for the type of startup she was building. When we got to the end of the pitch I asked her what her plans were for the $1 million. She froze and couldn't answer. She had spent so much time *building* the company that she didn't spend any time thinking about how to *grow* the company.*

There's no right or wrong answer to these questions—your company is your vision. How are you translating your vision into a plan for growth and how does money help you execute this plan? How much does your company currently spend each month to reach your current OKRs? If you scaled your OKRs by ten times, how much would it cost? How long does it take to build the next version of your product and how much would it cost to get the talent to accomplish this? How much does a solid marketing firm cost and how will they help you achieve some of your core OKRs?

Use the answers to the above questions to give you a baseline on how

---

*TL;DR I did eventually invest in her company.

you will use the investment. You may find after going through this exercise that you may need more investment (or sometimes less).

4. What Is the Smallest Amount of Money You Can Take and Still Get the Results You Want?

When taking outside money, you want to take as little as possible to get your business to the next step. That's right: *as little as possible*. It's counterintuitive, I know, but if you take too much money without knowing why you're taking it and what specifically you'll be using it for, you may end up giving up more ownership or putting yourself in personal financial jeopardy without the potential for an upside return. Every time you take outside funding from, say, a source such as venture capital, you are selling off a portion of your company. The more you take in, the bigger proportion of your company you sell off and the more control you, as a business owner, lose.

Compare these two scenarios:

Scenario 1: You accept a million in investment to develop and test an idea that you just *know* will work . . . but you don't have a product, let alone product-market fit.

Scenario 2: You're taking in a million from VCs because you have the mechanisms in place to make your product go viral (and the proof that your product is a *hit*) and you have a path to $100 million in sales in the next few years. You know exactly how you will use this seed money to amp up your production to meet consumer demands.

So let's do the math.

In Scenario 1, if you take in a million dollars before you have product-market fit, you are looking at giving up a significant portion (possibly up to one third) of your company off the bat to a venture capitalist (not to mention a lot of control). *Remember*: You may need to raise additional funds later on, as well as carve out some equity for your first employees. Oftentimes this additional equity comes from your ownership (not from the investor). So the more equity you give out now, the bigger the reduction in your equity in future fundraising rounds. Totaled, this could mean that right from the beginning, 50 percent of your business is owned by people other than you . . . and you don't even know if your product works yet. Talk about some *expensive* money!

Now consider Scenario 2. Since your product is already proven, already generating some revenue, you will have a bit more room to negotiate with potential investors for a higher valuation for your company. You can negotiate because your company has proven product-market fit (remember this!) and the risk to the investor has been reduced because there is proof that there's a market for what you're building.*

Types of Funding

You've gone through all the internal processing and questioning and you've come to the conclusion that, yes, funding is the right decision at this juncture. Now the question becomes, what *type* of funding is right for your business model?

There's no free money. Even if the money seems free (oh gee, I got a grant), no matter if it comes from a for-profit or a nonprofit institution, there's an expectation attached to it. As I've written earlier, in general,

---

*Valuation is an estimate of what your company is "worth." In terms of investment, your company's valuation is often used to justify the amount a venture capitalist invests in your company. It's important to note that your valuation often differs greatly from the value of your company if you were to sell it today. Remember: your company's true worth is only what someone is willing to pay for it—whether it be via stock or purchase by another company.

there are two types of funding for your business: non-equity based and equity based. It's best to think of these two types in terms of what you give up in exchange for the capital. In the case of non-equity-based funding, you get capital and in exchange you might pay a fee (like interest) or be a part of a marketing campaign (like many business-related grants from for-profit institutions). In the case of equity-based financing, you get capital and in exchange you give ownership in your company. Usually this ownership is until the business experiences a liquidity event (you sell it or you list your company on the public markets) or until it meets an unfortunate death.

Yes, there's no such thing as *free* money.

The Top Six Types of Funding for Builders

Okay, so technically there are way more than six types of funding, but we're going to focus on the ones commonly used by Builders to scale their companies. Some are pretty straightforward (personal finance, bank loans) and others, like crowdfunding and venture capital, will need to be explored in greater detail.

TYPE OF FUNDING		AMOUNT AVAILABLE	PROS/CONS	WORKS BEST...
Non-equity-based financing				
	Personal funds	$–$$	**Pros:** You're not tied to anyone else's bank account so you have complete control of your company at all times. **Cons:** You are personally liable. You can burn through all of your personal savings, your retirement, and rack up an incredible amount of personal debt if your business fails. And remember, a lot *do* fail. So, if you put all of your personal finances into one basket, then you are putting your future livelihood (and that of your family) at risk.	If you're in the beginning stages of developing an MVP and working through your business model. It's also great if you're a small business with solid revenue (meaning you make more than you spend) that is not looking at scaling your operations to become a bigger company.
	Friends and family	$–$$$	**Pros:** These are people who genuinely want the best for you. They want you to succeed and they need little proof from you about your model. Essentially, because they have a personal relationship with you, they are investing in *you* as a person. You do not need to convince them that you're going to return x, y, and z amounts of money within so many years. Overall, the pressure to prove your business is lower. **Cons:** Failure could destroy your personal relationship. You will find yourself on the receiving end of a lot of random phone calls and emails from distant relatives and people in your community—all eager to share their opinion on your business. Also, many of us are the "friends and family," the people everyone else turns to for financial support, so this might not be an option for Builders.	For Builders who have a large network of friends and family who would all be willing to pitch in small amounts. This method of funding isn't just for those people who come from ultra-rich families who are willing to give them a giant loan of $100,000 on demand.
	Grants	$$–$$$	**Pros:** You don't have to pay them back, and they often come with other benefits like marketing and PR support. They can also lead to great networking opportunities. **Cons:** The application process can be quite tedious and governed by politics. You might have to engage an outside consultant to help you develop your application, particularly for government grants.	For founders with strong writing skills and the ability to manage the application process. Builders with experience writing grants for a nonprofit can translate that experience to writing business grants.

TYPE OF FUNDING		AMOUNT AVAILABLE	PROS/CONS	WORKS BEST...
	Bank loans and credit cards	$$–$$$$	**Pros**: The nice thing about loans is that unlike friends and family, crowdfunding, angels, or VCs, you are not beholden to anyone else's ideas or concepts for your business. The bank is not your boss and you usually have a great deal of flexibility in how you use the capital. The repayment terms and conditions are set at the beginning of the loan, so you know from the outset exactly how much you're getting, what your interest rate is, and when you have to pay it back. Credit cards are even more flexible and can be used quickly, especially if you need a short-term bridge while waiting for other types of funding or revenue. **Cons**: You assume all the risk, which means if the business fails, you are personally responsible for paying the amount back. You're dealing with a bank and not someone personally invested in the success of your business. If you don't have solid credit, cash flow, or a business plan, you can forget about securing a bank loan. Credit cards are often an extremely expensive form of money, some charging up to 30% percent interest if you don't pay off your entire balance every month.	Bank loans: For Builders with a credit score above 700, a decent cash flow in the business, and an asset like a house. Credit cards: For Builders with a less-than-perfect credit score and who need capital to make purchases and have the ability to pay off balances prior to the bills' due dates.
Both non-equity- and equity-based financing				
	Crowd-funding	$$–$$$	**Pros**: Great if you have a large, active network that is ready to support you and already online. **Cons**: There are risks. Especially if you do an all-or-nothing model. If the campaign fails, you are DOA. Also your networks need to be fairly tech savvy as all of these platforms are managed online. Additionally, depending on how much you raise, you could be looking at racking up a pretty big accounting fee at the end of the year ... as well as quite a few people who literally have their nose in your business.	For Builders with large networks and communities that are already online. Crowdfunding platforms are a great way to engage family and friends who aren't active investors.

TYPE OF FUNDING		AMOUNT AVAILABLE	PROS/CONS	WORKS BEST...
Equity-based financing				
	Angel investors	$$–$$$$	**Pros:** Angel investors may choose to invest in startups in the very beginning stages before other investors like VCs are even willing to look at them. If you've got a great idea but not a lot of business history or profits to back it up, an angel might be an angel for you. **Cons:** It's common for angels to start small and increase their investments over time. Also angel investors might not be experienced investors, which might mean that you will not only have to manage your company, but staff as well.	For Builders who are relatively new to fundraising and are looking for early money (pre-revenue) for their company.
	Venture capital	$$$–$$$$	**Pros**: Investors assume the risk, meaning low personal financial risk to you. Larger amounts are available and most are "patient," meaning not looking for quick returns. If you decide to raise more money, they can also invest more (called follow-on) in addition to their initial investment. **Cons:** Venture capital can be very hard for Builders to get as it's often based on networks and track record. There are few VCs of color and women investors. At the early stage, network becomes very important as you might not have a track record yet. Companies accepting venture capital are often expected to sell their company (exit) or go for an initial public offering (IPO).	For Builders starting high-growth companies (shooting for a value of $500 million or more) that they plan to sell or put on the public stock market (through an IPO).

1. Personal Funds

Basically, this is where, as the name implies, you use your own funds from your own savings, retirement accounts, or credit cards. I suggest using your personal funds when you are at the very, very beginning of building your company as it gives you a bit more flexibility, since your only stakeholder is yourself. Note: Dig into your success toolbox (Step 2) and use the exit number you calculated. If you find yourself heading into more than 100 percent of your exit number and you're starting to generate revenue, then that could be a signal to bring in other partners.

> ### Builder Trap: Using Your Personal Credit Cards
>
> The problem with using personal credit cards for your startup is that it can be incredibly risky for people not already in the financial system. For starters, the debt limit on your personal credit cards is based on your current credit score. If you haven't been able to establish your credit or have bad credit, your limit may be way too small to reasonably use a personal card to fund your startup. Secondly, if you use a credit card to pay your startup costs, you may end up with a very high balance. Carrying too much debt on that credit card could mean that you won't be eligible for other forms of business funding. And, most importantly, using a personal credit card means that *you* are the one on the hook if your startup fails and you need to pay off that very high balance.
>
> Now that I've scared you, credit cards can be an effective financial tool *if you manage them correctly*. Most credit cards offer fraud protection, and that can be useful if you are making a ton of online purchases or you're traveling.* Credit cards can also be very useful when you need a short-term bridge loan (less than fifteen days) while waiting for a payment from a vendor to clear. Only use your credit cards in this way if the payment you're waiting for is coming from a trusted vendor with a track record of timely payments.

---

*Never, ever get a credit card without fraud protection.

2. Friends and Family

Calling these people "friends and family" is a bit of a misnomer. Yes, it can include family and friends, but this can also include anyone in your network who would be willing to contribute to your business. It could be your aunt's best friend Sasha, who thinks, "Oh! I've known Alex since they were a baby. I want to invest in their new business!"

> **Tool: Utilizing Your Personal Advisory Board**
>
> This is where you may want to recruit a member of your personal advisory board to run a little "pass interference," so to speak. Give them some talking points so you don't have to explain to Cousin Sasha for THE FIFTH TIME that overnight successes are not really a thing. My mother, aka "the drama whisperer," who is a very important member of my personal advisory board, does this for me all the time.

Keep in mind that your friends and family can invest in you and your business using methods other than direct financial contributions. Your family and friends could save you money through actions. For example, say you decided to move back in with a family member for a few months in the nascent stages of building your business. That could save you thousands of dollars. Even though your family isn't writing a direct check, it is an investment in your business by proxy. And that can be just as valuable, if not even more so.

When I first moved to Atlanta to scale DID, my husband and I both were working around the clock, and it was difficult to find great childcare for my son, who was then a baby.

We were extremely lucky to have a care service via my husband's company, and so we put him in the local nursery school. This nursery school wasn't great. It was the kind of place where overworked parents dumped their kids with overworked and underpaid staff for ten hours a day. There was one kid with a permanent snot-crusted nose who was there every day before we arrived and every day after we left. Every morning, when I dropped my son off, he would look at me with his big brown eyes as if to say, "Girl, you are sooo wrong for leaving me here." The kid with the snotty nose would look at me as if to say, "When you come get him, take me with you." It broke my heart.

Exhausted, exasperated, and carrying a whale-sized load of maternal guilt, I called up my mom, telling her, "I don't know what to do. I just can't leave him there anymore!" My mom, God bless her, asked me if I'd like her to come. I agreed, thinking she'd maybe spend a week or two while we got back on our feet. But no, that wonderful woman packed up her bags and left Santa Fe permanently to move across the country and help save my son from the same crusty-nosed fate of his peers.

My mom didn't give me money. She gave me something much more valuable: peace of mind. She was a widow living the high-desert retiree life in New Mexico and she gave it all up to come help me and my family. I knew, always, that my son was getting the food, love, and care that he needed. For all you parents out there, you know the struggle (and the expense!) of getting decent childcare. Without my mom, my business might not have made it. Personally, I don't think I would have made it either.

I encourage you to be creative in thinking about how you can lean on your community for this kind of "money that's not money." Even if you don't have kids, or your parents don't have the space for you to move back in, there are plenty of other ways that friends and family members can help.

For example, a founder friend of mine is the child of immigrant parents from Costa Rica and Guatemala. As a first-generation American, she went to a big Ivy League school, got a big fancy job at a big fancy company . . . and then risked it all to pursue entrepreneurship.

My friend's parents had no idea what she was doing—her mom was a housekeeper and her dad had a landscaping company.* Despite her parents' confusion, however, they supported her. Every time my friend had to travel for her company, she'd come home and her place would be clean and there'd be fresh food in her fridge. Her parents weren't giving her a blank check, but their care saved her money on takeout food and her time on cleaning and it showed her love when she was tired and striving and risking everything.

3. Grants

Business grants are the closest thing to free money you will find. Usually relatively small in dollar amount (most are under $50,000, although there are some that are much higher) and nonrenewable (you are only able to receive the money once), grants can be a great way to get the necessary funding to build out the early version of your product without giving up any equity in your company.

There are two primary groups that distribute grants for businesses: foundations/nonprofits/nongovernmental organizations (NGOs) and the government. Each has its own application process and time requirements, though foundation grants usually are a bit easier to apply for than government grants, which often require outside letters of support. Gov-

---

*Obviously my friend's mom and dad were both successful entrepreneurs and deeply influenced my friend's entrepreneurship journey. However, like many people of color, they didn't self-identify as the badass Builders that they are because the marketing of entrepreneurship/startups is around the fields that most white men find valuable.

ernment grants, however, tend to be for more money and are often renewable.

Foundation/Nonprofit Business Grants

There are a number of foundations, nonprofits, and NGOs that provide grants to those building businesses. Some grants are unrestricted, like the Doonie Fund—meaning you can use the money in any way you see fit—and some have restrictions and rules and may require you to pay them back if your company reaches a certain revenue threshold. Also, microlending platforms like Kiva and Grameen are great resources for early capital.

Government Business Grants

Grants.gov hosts a database of federally sponsored grants, including ones for small businesses. The application process requires your business to be registered with the U.S. government and have a DUNS number (a unique nine-digit identification number). State-level small business grants are generally open to companies that focus on regional concerns. You can search for grants in your own state and industry by looking at your state's department of commerce website or grants portal.

On a global level, several countries have grants and loan programs earmarked that provide capital to small businesses. In the UK, the government maintains a portal with information on small business finance programs around the country, including a link to apply for a government-backed startup loan of up to £25,000.*

---

*The portal is located at www.gov.uk/business-finance-support. It has a LONG list of small business financing programs, some countrywide and others city specific.

The Doonie Fund: How I Invest in Other Black Women Entrepreneurs with Microgrants

Like most people I really struggled when we were first hit with the pandemic. One moment I was flying back and forth between Atlanta and New York and prepping for a family trip to Alaska in April, and then I was stuck at home with a bored four-year-old with a strange obsession with nineties club music.

As the head of an organization with two locations and more than twenty staff members, there wasn't a lot of space for me to actually be human when the pandemic first started. People were depending on me and I had to act fast. Several of the founders in digitalundivided's programs were experiencing extreme distress because the shutdown happened so quickly. Furthermore, Black entrepreneurs, especially Black women entrepreneurs, were having difficulty acquiring loans due to the inequity in the federal Paycheck Protection Program (PPP), which highlighted the existing inequities in the U.S. banking system. I quickly authorized thousand-dollar grants to them, which digitalundivided was able to distribute in forty-eight hours. I didn't ask permission. I just did it because it needed to be done and I could do it. If someone had a problem with it, I would handle that later.

The impact of not asking permission to do something that needed to be done was extremely empowering for me. Sometimes as Builders we don't understand our own power, because again we're told that the race can only be run one way. Here's the thing about times of great challenge: they create enormous opportunity.

I took the refund from Alaska Cruise (aka the vacation that will never ever happen) and started the Doonie Fund (TDF), named after my maternal grandmother, Kathryn "Doonie" Hale, who was a fashion entrepreneur in Milwaukee.* The goal was to give out hundred-dollar microinvestments to one hundred Black women entrepreneurs.

The Doonie Fund investment criteria are straightforward. Potential recipients have to (a) self-identify as a Black woman, (b) work on their business full-time, and (c) have an established web presence (an active website, Shopify site, Instagram, etc.). The fund is purposely frictionless as I firmly believe that Black women know what's best for their businesses. Investments are distributed directly into the entrepreneurs' accounts within days.

One Medium post, a few emails, and six weeks later, the fund grew to more than $160,000, providing microinvestments to over 1,600 Black-women-owned businesses. In 2021, TDF distributed an additional $50,000 in microinvestment grants. The fund takes a holistic approach to economic impact by investing in a wide variety of businesses. And a movement was born. The Doonie Fund inspired others to create their own funds, such as the Kitty Fund, started by the CEO of the fintech platform Founders First in honor of her mother, and the Pittsburgh-based Phoenix Fund.

My mom, my friend's parents, and funds like the Doonie Fund illustrate the power that the Builder community has at our fingertips.

4. Bank Loans and Credit Cards

Bank loans and credit cards are the most basic form of getting capital for your company. However, these forms of capital can be very difficult and very costly for Builders because you start to incur fees, namely interest charges, from the very moment you sign on the dotted line.

---

*In the Black community, everyone has a nickname.

Bank Loans

A bank loan should theoretically be simple. You borrow a sum of money from the bank to start your business. Then you pay it back to the bank over a period of years with interest. Interest rates are set by individual banks and generally take into account the borrower's credit score, as well as what interest rates are nationwide.

But even qualifying for a bank loan can be extremely difficult for Builders who are just starting their first business, especially those who have been traditionally locked out of the financial ecosystem. In order to get a bank loan, you'll have to figure out how to jump through enough hoops to have the following:

- A business that is already established. Most online lenders require that it be operational for at least a year, and traditional brick and mortar banks want two years.
- A minimum annual revenue of anywhere from $50,000 to $250,000.
- A good personal credit score. In the United States, lenders often want at least a score of 680 before they'll consider you for a business loan.

If you don't have a high enough credit score, banks may work with you anyway, but their interest rates may be drastically higher. Also many banks require a personal guarantee, which means that if your business cannot pay back its loan on time, the bank can come after you personally and seize any assets you have, including your house or car.

Microloans

One option for Builders outside of a traditional bank loan can be a microloan. These are short-term loans from nonprofits like Accion. They do not require your business to be as established as bank loans do, making them useful for startups. But their APR (the interest rate you pay) can often be higher and, as the name implies, they only provide small amounts of money. The average microloan is about $13,000.

When I started my first company, The Budget Fashionista, Accion was the only funding option that was available for me (besides credit cards). Again, this was before venture capital, and even private equity, was really available to Black women founders. In 2007, Accion was willing to assume the risk of loaning me money for my online business when other banks didn't see the value of an online site or even understand how it worked. I went on to receive three loans from Accion, which were crucial in helping me scale my company.

You've determined that your company is growing by leaps and bounds. So much that you need a substantial amount of unrestricted money to be able to capitalize on the market opportunity. You need equity investment. So how do you catch the eye of an investor? I share some tips below.

How to Attract Investors

Really think through *how* you are going to make those returns on the investments. Not just on the level of "a customer buys a product, then you make and send said product," but in the big-picture sense. How are you going to ensure that you see x percent of growth quarter over quarter? What is the minimum turnover you'd need from each sale? Which additional revenue streams will you set up to ensure a safety net of consistent income? Which of those multiple revenue streams will you prioritize?

How do you do that if you didn't go to Yale or have contacts down at the yacht club?

Share What You Know

Social media platforms like Medium, Twitter, LinkedIn, and Clubhouse and podcasting sites YouTube and Stitcher are great places to share your insights about your business and start to gain traction as a voice in your industry. The more people become familiar with your voice, the more likely investors can trust that you have the authority, presence, and commitment to excel in your entrepreneurial endeavors. This is how I was able to raise over $5 million for Genius Guild prior to its launch.

Of course, at this point maybe you don't have the expertise... but that doesn't mean you can't research.

Be the Hunter

A big part of entrepreneurship is proactivity. That's why, especially as a newer entrepreneur and a Builder, you will most likely find yourself needing to reach out to investors.

But there is an *art* to it.

First and foremost, find the *right people* to reach out to. If there is a top investor who you are aware of and whose work you've followed regularly, reach out to them. If you aren't aware of any investors, it's time to do your research. Get on social media. Most VCs hang around Twitter and LinkedIn. Ask your entrepreneurial friends. Seek out articles, podcasts, and books to find the top VCs for your industry. The more reconnaissance you can do before the approach, the better. Don't just do mass cold-call reach-outs to VCs you only have a passing familiarity with. Be selective about who you really want on your team.

Second, *perfect the task*. I'm often baffled by some of the bland, impersonal email I receive from entrepreneurs seeking investors. Trust me, if you just came across my name thirty seconds before sending me a message, I can tell.

Here are my three rules for reaching out to investors:

- **1. Appeal to the ego . . . but don't be corny about it.**

    Entrepreneurial hopefuls reach out to me on a daily basis. If they start with something like, "I just want to connect with you," then I pretty much always hit the delete button and move on to the next message. But if they share that they've read something I've written or was a part of the Doonie Fund, I almost always read the email.

    Aim for something like, "Hey, Kathryn, I've been following your career since The Budget Fashionista days. I just read your piece on Medium last month about racial profiling in investments and I was really inspired by x, y, and z points. Here's what I'm working on . . ."

    You don't have to be a fangirl (or person) and say you read my fifth-grade book report. But show that you've at least googled me and have a general understanding of who I am besides a person who writes checks.

- **2. Find a genuine point of connection.**

    What do you and they have in common? Basket weaving? Curling? Even if you don't have an obvious commonality, you can be creative and find a connection with almost anything. Say you're building a nutrition company and you heard recently on a podcast that your target VC is an avid powerlifter. Use this connection to build a bridge to the VC.

Tip: While college is a connection point, if you went to a large school, it's a pretty broad connection point. Try to be as specific as possible (without being awkwardly personal, of course).

One more tip: Make sure whatever connection point you make has a positive association with that person. Say you both lived in Bangkok. Find some evidence that your target investor actually enjoyed their experience living in Bangkok. If they said in an interview that they hated it, and you say you loved it, how do you think reminding them of it will make them feel?

3. Don't shy away from sending free products!

Everyone loves free swag.

True story: An entrepreneur emailed me and said, "I heard you the other day talking on a podcast about the challenge of finding great hair care products for braids. I have a hair company you might be interested in and I'd love to send you some free samples." I was definitely interested—so was my COO—and we tried it and we loved it. That company is now in the pipeline for investment from our company.

Word to the wise: Don't put any conditions on the gift. It should simply be a gift.

Builder Trap: Asking for Money Too Soon

There's an old saying: "If you ask for money, you get advice. If you ask for advice, you get money."

STEP 6: GETTING THE BAG

> This is true for investment as well. While you should definitely share that you're fundraising and the amount, DO NOT ask for an investment at the first meeting. Imagine if someone you *just* met asked you for $1 million? It would be weird. That being said, if the investor isn't moving your company forward with due diligence* by the third meeting, then it's probably best to move on. If you're unclear where you stand in the process, then feel free to ask the investors.

5. CROWDFUNDING

Crowdfunding and equity crowdfunding platforms (I call them crowdinvesting) are great ways to raise funds for your startup. Crowdfunding (think platforms like GoFundMe and Kickstarter) raises money from a group of people in exchange for a prize/product. This differs from crowdinvesting, which allows anyone the ability to invest a hundred dollars or more in exchange for equity in your startup. Crowdinvesting is an excellent tool for Builders as it allows you to utilize your network, rather than focus on gaining access to gatekeepers.

How to Win at Crowdfunding

In the early part of 2015, I was exhausted and ready to move on from digitalundivided. We had just completed the initial analysis of what was the first ProjectDiane report and the number of Black women in the

---

*Investopedia defines "due diligence" as "an investigation, audit, or review performed to confirm facts or details of a matter under consideration." Basically it's a focused review of your documents from financials to contracts, to make sure the potential investor or partner understands all the risks associated with investing in your company.

193

startup space was very low, so low that it was obvious the work to change the landscape was going to be super difficult.

We thought a documentary, called *#ReWriteTheCode*, would be a great way to qualitatively share the results of #ProjectDiane with a larger audience and turned to Kickstarter to raise the funds. We spent close to a month planning the campaign and then *TechCrunch* released a report on the gender breakdown of Crunchbase (we speculate that the press #ProjectDiane received was one of the things that nudged them along).* We were forced to change our campaign to just focus on the documentary element.

The purpose of the campaign was twofold—to raise money to produce *#ReWriteTheCode* and give a final, positive farewell to our community. I set the goal for our one-month campaign low, $25,000, because we didn't know what to expect, as crowdfunding and crowdinvesting were fairly new.

I raised over $50,000 in less than forty hours. By the end of the campaign I had raised close to $100,000 across two platforms.

I learned A LOT from running this successful campaign. Here are some of my tips:

Time to Call Your College Roommate

The single best piece of advice I can offer about running a successful crowdfunding campaign is to build a strong network prior to launch, especially for campaigns in which there isn't a tangible product or if your product isn't "sexy," like, say, a cloud storage platform. People are investing/donating/pledging because they believe in your idea and, in most cases,

---

*The business publication *Fast Company* did a report in March 2015 on the work I was doing to document the lack of diversity in the startup world. Soon after this article was published, Crunchbase started to track the diversity metrics of those in their database. See https://www.fastcompany.com/3044066/inside-the-campaign-to-disrupt-techs-huge-diversity-problem and https://about.crunchbase.com/blog/new-crunchbase-diversity-spotlight/.

STEP 6: GETTING THE BAG

because they believe in you. The people who believe in you are the people who actually know you.

In order for your campaign to be successful, you will need to access EVERY network you've ever been part of: your weekend basketball league, your college alumni association, your mom's church usher board, and your Ultimate Frisbee team. Everyone.

More than 32 percent of our campaign backers came from my personal network. Twenty-eight percent of the people who pledged (172 backers) came from either my private Facebook friend group (70 backers out of 72 friends) or a curated Friends of Kathryn list of 135 people. The FOKers are people I have a direct, personal connection with, meaning people I consider friends in the pre-IG-Facebook sense of the word. We segmented those folks out, and I sent emails directly to them from my personal email account using a mail merge tool. As a result, over 79 percent of my personal network supported the campaign.

However, your networks shouldn't all receive the same message or even the same message via the same platform. Segmenting your contacts is VITAL to a successful campaign because it helps you tailor your message to different groups based on your relationship. Your college roommate shouldn't receive the same email as the people who subscribe to your newsletter.

For example, a number of my friends are allergic to email. I could send them an invite to LeBron James's house for Christmas with a white elephant gift exchange led by Oprah and they wouldn't open the invite because it was sent via email. So for those people, I literally texted the request via my mobile phone with a direct link to our campaign page. One hundred percent of those people pledged.

You're Going to Need Some Time

It takes a solid two months, at a bare minimum, to set up a successful campaign, as you will need time to prepare your network for your "ask," the amount you will need them to donate. I know that two months is like two years in online world time, but you really need that time to prepare your network for the big campaign. You don't need a big network to raise money on crowdfunding platforms. HOWEVER, you do need people who are ready to support you financially. If you don't currently have these people in your network, spend a bit of time developing this network prior to the campaign. Start by joining and becoming an active member of a few Facebook groups of those who are interested in your product/service. Reach out to your local high school/college alumni network and ask if you could share information on your company (NOT the crowdfunding campaign).

In order to win at crowdfunding, you must give potential backers/investors solid reasons why they should invest in you (actually list them out) and remind them of the return they will get from investing in your campaign. Why is your company important? What is the growth potential? How will the supporter be entertained or enlightened or educated?

The most frequent reason we heard from our backers as to why they invested in our campaign is that we made them feel good about giving and that we framed the project as something *bigger than themselves.*

People want to believe in the power of community, they want to believe in *you*. Make them believe.

Prep Your Friends

To really win at crowdfunding, you MUST prep your network at least ONE MONTH prior to the campaign's actual launch date. I informed our networks, both personal and general, about one month prior to launching our campaign. We then sent one email per week leading up to the campaign with a daily email starting three days prior to launch. This gave our backers a chance to prepare. Several people told me that they gave higher pledges because they were able to put the amount into that month's budget.

Those early messages are super important because you need your network to be ready to move *at the launch* of the campaign. According to Kickstarter, the most successful campaigns raise at least 50 percent of their goals in the first forty-eight hours. It's much easier to raise that initial amount from those who know you and your work than from complete strangers. We also learned that asking for a specific amount is especially effective, as most people are super busy. We asked our friends for $500, and 18 of the 132 FOKers did at least $500, and several did even more.

Tool: Crowdfunding Draft Email

Here's a draft template of the first email we sent out to the FOKers list. Feel free to use this as a template for your own emails. (Seriously . . . go ahead and use it.)

Hey ‹insert name›,

Today, we're launching our ‹insert platform› campaign to ‹insert name of campaign›!
 We're raising ‹insert $$$› to ‹insert why you're raising money›. Click here to join ‹insert hyperlink›.
 Three Super Awesome Reasons you should ‹support/invest› in our company:
  ‹Reason 1›
  ‹Reason 2›

> \<Reason 3\>
>
> Need more reasons? Read this awesome \<describe source\>: \<insert blog post, article, etc. about your idea or product\>.
>
> **How you can help right now:**
>
> 1. Invest TODAY! While ALL investments are appreciated (seriously, we appreciate all amounts), we're asking for an investment of \<insert amount\> from all our friends.
>
> 2. Spread the word. Let your friends know about the upcoming campaign.
>
> 3. Please tweet away. Here's a tweet that you can use:
>
> (this needs to be NO LONGER THAN 140 characters) \<short opening\>\<insert what you're doing\>. Support the \<hashtag\> campaign TODAY. More here: \<insert shortened link\>.
>
> We're so very excited about the campaign and look forward to having your support as we GO BIG to solve this problem.
>
> Feel free to shoot me any questions directly at \<insert your email\>.
>
> \<Insert Awesome Closing\>,
> \<Your Wonderful Name\>

Your network isn't just for pledges, but also for advice. We were lucky that we had friends who had just completed a super successful Kickstarter campaign that raised over $150,000 for a fifty-state tour promoting LGBTQ rights. Of the many excellent pieces of advice Taryn and Peter gave us, the one that stood out was that you should wait at least twenty-four hours after sending details to your targeted list before contacting your general mailing list.

Why? No one wants to be the first investor. You want your general list to see that you already have support and momentum, and if they don't invest, they will miss out on a good thing.*

For outreach to our general database, we used a newsletter service, Mailchimp, which allowed us to segment and create new lists based on response rates. Mailchimp also served as a stand-in customer relationship management system (CRM), which helped us manage responses to questions and track interest in the campaign based on who was opening our email updates.† We further segmented our general list based on how we met the subscriber—Was it from a conference? Did they attend an event? In total, we had over twelve lists—some with thousands of contacts and some with only ten. This allowed us to not only see the open rate by point of contact, but also which group had more of an affinity to our messaging. We sent out the first email (to twelve lists) and then we created two more lists—those who opened the email and those who didn't. We wrote targeted messages to those who opened the email (obviously they were interested) and focused on getting those who did not open to open the next one.

The conversion rate (the number of people who donated as a result of receiving the newsletter) for our newsletter list was about 9 percent, which seems to be a pretty standard conversion rate for a crowdfunding campaign, although it's hard to tell because there's not much information to compare it to.

Choose the Right Platform

The platform you use can make or break your project. Choosing the correct platform is based on the goals for your project. I would strongly

---

*Speaking of which, thank you to Peter and Taryn for being our first backers!
†Frankly, we had zero interest in learning how to use a CRM.

suggest choosing a well-known platform because you need to spend your time selling your idea to your network, NOT educating them on how to use a new platform.

We chose a popular platform (Kickstarter) to run the initial campaign because we knew that a majority of our network had at least heard of it, and we wanted to know if there was a market for what we were doing. A successful crowdfunding campaign can be a great indicator that your product has great product-market fit. The thought process was simple: Why would we make a documentary if no one wanted to see it? Kickstarter also offered a great back end that really let us see where our pledges were coming from (over 29 percent from Twitter) and what the average dollar amount was.

1. **Is it all-or-nothing or flexible?** All-or-nothing means you set a goal. If you reach that goal, congrats! You get the whole bag of cash. If not, you walk away with nada. Flexible, of course, means that you get to keep whatever you make. Here's the catch, though: with flexibility, if you don't reach your goal there's often a penalty in fees that you need to pay. Read the fine print.
2. **Equity, rewards, or donation?** Crowdfunding sites generally give three options for investors. Either you can give a charitable donation out of the goodness of your heart, you can give an investment in exchange for a reward such as being first in line for the new product, or you can get equity and get a small stake in the company.
3. **What are the fees?** Crowdfunding sites take a percentage of your earnings—usually somewhere between 3 and 10 percent. Be on the alert for penalty fees and taxes that you'll need to pay. This is especially important to think about if you run a campaign late in the year. If you make a lot of money via

crowdfunding in the late fall but don't make money from your business until the spring of next year, you will be hit *hard* on taxes without any deductible income. If you're outside the United States, make sure to check if there are any additional fees charged for non–U.S. based campaigns.

4. **Is the site Reg A+, Reg D, or Reg CF?** In 2012, Obama signed the JOBS Act into law, allowing startups to raise capital via crowdfunding without having to go through the big hassle and even bigger expense of registering their capital with the Securities and Exchange Commission. Now, depending on your funding goal, you will want to do a little research into which one is right for you, but here's a quick rundown*:

   - **Reg A+:** Anyone can invest. There are two tiers: Tier 1 caps at $20 million and Tier 2 caps at a cool $50 million. If you get into Tier 2 territory, you're looking at some pretty high accounting and legal costs . . . as well as ongoing reporting.
   - **Reg D:** Similar to Reg A+ but only open to accredited investors (although it will allow up to thirty-five nonaccredited investors for a cost . . . a big cost that comes with a big headache). This generally applies to angel investors (we'll get back to them in a bit).
   - **Reg CF:** Anyone can invest but it caps at $5 million. The good news is that you have lower costs and fewer disclosure requirements.

---

*If outside the United States, make sure to research similar categorizations/restrictions in your country.

Setting Your Campaign Goal

The importance of setting the correct goal can't be underestimated. Set it too low, and you won't be able to complete the project; set it too high, and you won't be able to raise enough to trigger the success threshold. Set your goal for the base amount you want to raise plus an additional 20 to 25 percent for other costs and fees.

How to Figure Out Your Campaign Goal

1. **Start with your base goal.** This is super important because you need to ask for what you really need, but you also don't want to overshoot your goal.
2. **Then add fees (at least 20 percent of your base amount).** Crowdfunding campaigns are a business. An amazing business (no, really, they're very good), but a business nonetheless. As a result they charge a number of fees. Add an additional 15 to 20 percent to your campaign goal to cover them.
3. **Add the cost of staff (8 percent of the base amount).** You're going to need help. It's very, very hard to run a successful crowdfunding campaign without help from a team. You will need to follow up on emails, send direct tweets, and do other important outreach, which is impossible for one person to do alone. If you don't have a team or staff, then look at services like Upwork and Fiverr to hire temporary support staff.*

---

*We raised our entire goal in the first forty hours of the campaign, because we had a team of *four* people working pretty much around the clock for the first forty-eight hours.

The Video (You Really Have to Do This)

Companies with videos get funded more often (50 percent) than projects without (30 percent). So having a video (no longer than two minutes) is important. Don't spend much money on this; you can literally record it on your iPhone with a ten-dollar ring light.

On a basic level, your crowdfunding video should cover the following:

- Tell viewers who you are and about your company
- Tell viewers the story behind your company
- Explain your product
- Explain why your company is a good investment
- Make a direct request for support and explain why they should support the campaign
- Thank them

6. Angel Investors

Angel investors are high-net-worth individuals who invest in startups in exchange for equity. They typically have an already successful career and are focused on giving back to the industries. They may or may not have a history in the startup world, but that does not make them any less valuable. Keep in mind that they are investing their own money. Generally, angel investors fall into three categories:

- **High-net-worth individuals:** $1 million in liquid assets
- **Very-high-net-worth individuals:** $5 million in liquid assets
- **Ultra-high-net-worth individuals:** $30 million in liquid assets

Where do you find angel investors? While they used to be hard to find, with the advent of the internet and a little help from a global pandemic, angels are easier than ever to connect with.

You can also tap the angel capital network in your area to find local angel investors, as well as your college university network, since many also have angel networks. Angels tend to have an emotional investment in their projects and, like crowdfunding, invest in the *individual* as well as the company.

7. Venture Capital

Venture capital firms invest in startups with high growth potential and make investments on behalf of themselves or other investors in exchange for equity in the fund. My VC fund, Genius Guild's Greenhouse Fund, invests in exceptional Black founders building amazing companies that serve the Black community and beyond.

A venture capital fund is made up of two groups of people: the general partners (GPs) and the limited partners (LPs). The GPs manage the day-to-day activity of the fund and usually only contribute a small percentage of the fund's capital.* The LPs are high-net-worth individuals, families, foundations (like the Ford and Rockefeller Foundations) and university endowments, corporations, or pension funds like CalPERS, the pension fund for most state and local employees in California. These entities contribute most of the money in a fund but aren't involved in the day-to-day decisions.

Now, even though LPs put in the majority of the money, the GPs are who you are getting in bed with. These are the people you actually work with in building your company.

---

*The word "capital" in the world of VC means "money that can be invested."

It's helpful to think about GPs as fellow startup founders. The goal of GPs is to make a return for their limited partners over a given time period: usually three to five times back the original investment over ten years. Ideally, GPs want to start seeing some returns in year seven or eight.

So how do VCs actually make money? On top of a management fee (generally about 2 percent of the total amount under management of the fund annually), GPs also make money from the "carry," the profit that GPs keep after paying back the LPs' initial investment. Generally, after paying back LPs, 80 percent of what's remaining will go to the LPs and 20 percent will go to the GPs.

Tool: Understanding Venture Math

ABC Fund makes $1 million on an investment.

1. The fund first pays back its limited partners' investment of $900,000 in the fund, which leaves $100,000.
2. Of the $100,000 left, LPs get 80 percent (or $80,000) and you, the GP, get $20,000.

Now, here's the rub—about 75 percent of VC investments fail. Let's say a fund invests in ten companies—VCs expect that four will fail completely, three or four will return their investment (neither making nor losing money), and one or two will actually return more than the initial investment. This is why if you tell an investor you're building a $1 million company they give you a blank look. They are going to need you to guarantee a billion to recoup their losses and turn a profit for them.

> Venture capitalists invest based on potential. Can you become big quickly so that you turn their $1 million investment into a $10 million return back to them? For a Builder's company, however, that is an incredible amount of pressure. If your business isn't structured to scale rapidly, and you don't know how to allocate your funds efficiently, it will break under that pressure.
>
> At the end, when looking to invest in new projects, VCs typically ask themselves three questions:
>
> 1. How quickly can this business grow to the level that I can return the money my LPs invested in my fund?
> 2. Will I own enough of the company to get a return on investment?
> 3. Does this team have the capacity to succeed?

There are two primary documents venture capitalists use to invest in early-stage, pre-revenue companies: the simple agreement for future equity (SAFE) form and convertible notes.*

SAFEs: SAFEs were created in 2013 by the Silicon Valley–based accelerator program Y Combinator as a way for investors to quickly invest in pre-revenue companies without placing a ton of costly (and lengthy) legal requirements on the early-stage startup. Investors are essentially investing in a future round of fundraising, meaning they are investing money now that will convert into shares† in your company when you raise your next round, at a hopefully higher valuation.

In exchange for investing early and taking the risk, you give these

---

*There are other types of documents used, but 99.9 percent of venture capitalists stick with some form of these two documents.
†In the interest of keeping things simple, I use the terms "stock" and "share" interchangeably.

investors a discount, basically a break on the price they pay for their shares once you raise your next round. These discounts are usually expressed as a percentage (10 percent to 30 percent).

For example, let's say a VC invested $100 at $1 per share at the SAFE round with a 10 percent discount. When you raise your next round, that $1 the VC invested in your company now allows them to purchase $1.10 of shares in your next round. So instead of just owning 100 shares when you raise your next round, the VC owns 110 shares.

Convertible Notes: Convertible notes are essentially loans, aka debt instruments, that can convert into preferred stock of your company if you raise your next round within a given time period (usually twelve to twenty-four months). If for some reason you don't raise your next round within the given time period, the investor can elect to convert the note into a loan document at a previously determined interest rate (anywhere from 3 percent to 8 percent).

Which one is best for you? That's a difficult question to answer as it depends on the needs of your company. Some VCs prefer convertible notes because they are fairly easy to put together and offer additional protection for the investor to reclaim some of their investment since they are essentially a loan. SAFEs are pretty straightforward as well but can offer VCs a bit more rights, like the right to a board seat.* Regardless of what instruments you decide to use to fund your company, as stated in the previous step, make sure you have an attorney with experience reviewing and crafting early-stage investing documents on your team.†

---

*I HIGHLY recommend reading Brad Feld and Jason Mendelson's book, *Venture Deals: Be Smarter Than Your Lawyer and Venture Capitalist.* It's an excellent manual that goes much further in-depth about venture capital in general, but especially about these two types of funding documents.

†Seriously, DO NOT skimp on this. Many lawyers will tell you that they can review these documents, and most won't have a clue. Ask for references from previous startups and/or venture funds they've worked with. If they are reluctant to share references, run as fast as you can.

Builder Trap: Taking That Sweet VC Money Without Asking the Right Questions

Remember, one of the most powerful things you can do as a POC Builder is to say no to money. And if it's not the right deal, you *should* say no. How do you know if this venture capitalist is the right person to invest in your business? Ask the right questions.

Does this VC have the same goal for my company that I do? First and foremost, you need to make sure your potential VC is aligned with your core values and your vision for the company. This is YOUR company, not their company. Look for VCs who are investing in your vision and trust your ability to lead. VCs SHOULD NOT be actively involved in the day-to-day decision-making of your company. The best VCs provide help and assistance in areas where you need it. They also serve as great sounding boards and confidants to help you figure out solutions to problems.

Do I want to be around this person for the next five years? As soon as you take on a VC investment, you take on someone who you have to be accountable to. You are married to this person until the end of your company. Make sure to choose a VC who you feel has your back. You don't want to turn around one day to find you've got a knife stuck in it.

Some questions for assessing your VC:

- What are their core values?
- Are they respected by other VCs in the community?
- Can they navigate the inevitable "shit hitting the fan" moments that come with scaling a business?
- Could I have dinner with this person and not want to fake choking on a bread roll halfway through?

> **Am I giving away too much of my company for this deal?** It's easy to focus on the prize without looking at the price tag. Keep in mind what I wrote earlier: there's no such thing as free money. If you jump in before you understand the valuation of your business, you may find yourself in a position down the line where you've given up half your company before you've made back even half what you invested in it.
>
> Also, as an investor, I want my founders to own a healthy share of their company as it keeps them incentivized to continue to build. As a general rule, founders should try to maintain 75 to 80 percent of equity after pre-seed investment and 50 to 60 percent post-seed investment. Note: the more money you raise, the more equity you will have to give up.*

The Data Room

One of the first things you need to put together after your pitch deck (more on this in a few pages) is your data room, also called your doc room. Most experienced investors will ask to see it. The term sounds scarier than it actually is. The data room is simply a file that contains important information about your company that helps an investor decide whether or not to put money into your company. It can be as simple as a Google Drive or Dropbox folder.†

Think of your data room as the sales floor of your startup. You want

---

*There are other ways of maintaining control of your company besides just owning most of it, which frankly is hard to do when you start to enter higher stages of funding (Series A and above). You can have clauses that allow you to control board seats, ability to cash out some of your stock, etc.

†Since the data room contains confidential documents about your company, I suggest making sure you limit access to certain emails and disable the ability of others to download your database.

to disclose enough for the investor to make an informed decision, but you don't need to put everything in there.

What Should Be in Your Data Room

Founder biographies: Make sure you have detailed bios of each founder and co-founder. Note that this is NOT the time to be modest. Go ahead and brag on yourself. You might also want to include bios of other core team members.

Pitch deck: More on how to build your pitch deck later in the chapter. Add your most recent pitch deck.

Cap table: Your capital table, aka cap table, is simply a chart showing who owns your company, how much they own, when they bought it, and the type of ownership (shares) they have in your company, among other information. The bigger your company gets and the more investment you take in, the more complicated your cap table becomes. So in the early days your goal should be to keep it as simple as possible.

My advice is that before you even *think* about giving away your shares, construct what you see as your ideal cap table five years from now. Now think about this: your initial investors will not be your *only* investors. So if you give 30 percent of your company away to the first VC that comes along, you only have 10 percent for future investors . . . future investors you might really need to scale your business.*

---

*If you think you, as the founder, will own more than 50 percent of your company with VCs backing you, I am here to burst your bubble. After undergoing several rounds of funding, Mark Zuckerberg only owned 28 percent of Facebook at its IPO. Get used to giving up your shares.

Product: Basic information about your product (what it is, how it works, etc.). Include screenshots of the product, any positive user reviews, and access to your product if it's not yet public.

Your technology (aka stack): A detailed description of the technology you use to build and maintain your product. For example, if you're running an online media company, an example of a stack might be your content management system (e.g., WordPress) and the place where your website (domain) is hosted (e.g., Google Cloud). You should also include any future technical developments, such as planning to build your own servers.

Financials: Your profit and loss statement by month (if you have them). This will show your monthly burn rate (your revenue minus the amount you have from any investment).

Marketing plan: How you are going to reach customers and ensure growth. Include basic versions of your marketing plan.

Sales/traction: Any growth projections, your monthly growth rate, your customer retention rate.

The game is not to keep it all; the game is to keep as much as you can while keeping your company's end goals achievable.

The BIG Question When Considering Taking on VC

Ask yourself this: Would I rather be in near-complete control of my company and its direction but limit the amount of money I may make in the long term OR would I rather give up control to maybe make a much larger sum?

These are two very different paths, and the choice is all based on your comfort with risk. If you choose option A, the safer route, there are plenty of other funding avenues that we have already explored. If you choose option B, the riskier route, then VCs might be for you. Building a high-growth startup, the type of companies venture capitalists tend to invest in, is risky business. Keep in mind, I am not advocating for one over the other. VC definitely has its problems (yes, you, Voldemort of VC), but a great majority of VCs are good people trying to invest in good companies. I believe in the good that venture capital can do for startups. The point is that it *is* a choice.

Keep in mind that it is far easier to go from a lifestyle company to a scalable business than from a scalable business to a lifestyle company. Therefore, I only recommend going the VC route once you have clarity on how you will scale your company.

> **Builder Trap: Not All Money Costs the Same**
>
> If there's one thing to remember regarding venture capital investment—really any investment—it's that *not all money costs the same*. Before accepting money, think about what it's going to cost you IN ADDITION to the money. It is particularly important for Builders to think about this because many of us come from cash-poor backgrounds, in which

access to capital has been nonexistent. So the thought of turning down money because it's going to be too hard to manage the ancillary issues that may come with it can induce a ton of anxiety.

However, it's crucial that you get comfortable with the ability to say no to expensive money. Is it worth taking capital from a needy investor whose required daily financial reports distract you from your ability to build your product? Is it worth taking a loan from a bank where you have to go on an Arctic expedition every time you want to speak with a human being? As a CEO, your time is extremely valuable. Before accepting any money, make sure to talk with others who've recently received money from that individual or group.

Startup Story: Girlboss—A Parable of Funding

Sophia Amoruso had a killer business. She went from community college dropout to entrepreneur who built her vintage clothing store on eBay, Nasty Gal, into a cool $30 million online clothing mecca—all with no credit cards and, miraculously, no debt. Nasty Gal's sales jumped from $24 million in 2011 to over $100 million in 2012. That year, it was even named the fastest-growing retail company by *Inc.* magazine.

It goes without saying that Sophia had a great business model, great fundamentals, great metrics—all the greats that should have made her an undeniable titan in her industry. In 2016, *Forbes* included her in its list of America's richest self-made women; that same year, Nasty Gal filed for bankruptcy.

What the hell happened?

Venture capital happened.

Sophia had built a successful, tech-enabled business that investors were champing at the bit to sink their gold teeth into. They wanted it so bad that the VCs saved her the hard work of pitching and jumped into their Priuses (this was in the 2010s) to woo her.

Being a new business owner without much experience in the world of VC, Sophia jumped at the opportunity. So how did she end up bankrupt?

Sophia fell smack-dab into the Builder trap above: not all money costs the same. Like 99.9 percent of the world (including some venture capitalists), she didn't understand how venture capital works. Nine out of ten venture capital deals do not make back the money that investors put in. This means that in order for a deal to be a win for a venture firm, it needs to not just return the money the VC invested in it BUT also make the VCs enough money to compensate for all their failed investments.

Whew . . . talk about a situation.

In both media interviews and on her company blog, Sophia has described the pressure that came from taking VC money: "We raised $40 million in 2012 at a $330 million valuation, which put an unreasonable price on our head, scaring away future investors." As a former Nasty Gal employee explained in an interview with the website *Jezebel*, "I think when the investors came in there was a lot of pressure. Pressure for us to be bigger. They wanted more profit, they wanted more product, they wanted to expand." And Nasty Gal added the infrastructure to do just that, opening a 50,000-square-foot headquarters in downtown Los Angeles, a 500,000-square-foot fulfillment center so that it could distribute its products independently, and two retail locations where customers could sample the Nasty Gal style in person.

While unchecked growth may seem like a mantra for the venture-funded world of Silicon Valley tech, fashion companies are especially vulnerable to VC issues because of their fundamental differences from tech companies. Apparel companies require a tremendous amount of liquid capital. Whereas a company like Uber can exist on the market for twelve years (and counting) without turning a real profit outside of market valuation, fashion retailers need to quickly pay for physical products and must keep enough of them on hand so that they always have something new to entice customers and build brand loyalty.

According to Sophia, the VCs expected annual sales to more than quadruple in one year. She says, "That money and expectation were a real shock to the system. We hired 100 people almost immediately and made a growth plan without having a lot of data to back it. . . . Things became too complex too fast." Soon sales started dropping, to $85 million in 2014, and then $77 million in 2015, just as expenses were increasing in pursuit of rapid growth.

Lawrence Lenihan, the managing director of FirstMark Capital, attributes the VC need for too-rapid growth to Nasty Gal's downfall: "Investors are overfunding these niche companies and forcing them to grow too rapidly at an unsustainable level. As in the case of Nasty Gal, this has destroyed the very fiber of its success. Not everybody can be a Facebook, Google, or Amazon."

Nasty Gal had a slew of other documented problems, including lawsuits from employees who claimed the company discriminated against them and fashion designers who alleged that it stole their designs. However, a number of its issues stemmed from taking VC money that encouraged unsustainable growth. When you're under pressure to make up for not only your failures but the failures of others, you start to do stupid shit, like opening a 50,000-square-foot headquarters in downtown LA.

The expectations of her investors, the insane level of growth that all venture capitalists seem to expect from their investments, was fundamentally about the VC mindset. To make the VC system work, Sophia's business needed to be the "unicorn" that paid back not only their investment in Nasty Gal, but also all their other investments that failed.

Fortunately for Sophia, she wasn't playing at the *hardest* level and had an extra life or two.* So, while Nasty Gal filed for bankruptcy in 2016, she was able to transition those learnings into Girlboss, an online community platform.

Funding Rounds Explained

Fundraising activities for startups are usually grouped in time-boxed periods called "rounds." At each round, you set a specific amount of money you're looking to raise based on a predetermined valuation of your business. At the pre-seed and seed funding rounds, which often happen prior to your company generating any significant amounts of revenue, the valuation is often set in agreement with your first major investor (aka your lead). Here's a breakdown of the common fundraising rounds:

> **Pre-seed funding:** This is the funding at the very beginning stages of a company. This is the money you use for the MVP, the money you use to get the idea out of your head and onto paper. Generally, this money comes from your own pockets or close friends and family. Genius Guild also invests at this level. So do risk-taking angel investors.
>
> **Seed funding:** Seed funding ($1 million to $5 million), as the name implies, is essentially where you plant a financial seed so you can grow that tree of your business. This is your first round of asking for equity investments and usually comes after you have a consistent and growing base of

---

*It's hard out there for *all* women. Yes, a majority of venture funding was given to white women founders, *but* only 2.3 percent of venture funding in 2020 went to women as a whole.

customers or users. In this stage, you're probably looking at equity crowdfunding, angel investors, and maybe some small-scale VCs. Genius Guild invests at this level.

Series A funding: This is for companies that have a proven idea, incoming revenue, and a solid strategy that prove they are ready to scale their business. This funding usually comes from VCs and can net $2 to $15 million.

Series B funding: After companies have acquired Series A funding and started to scale, they may pursue additional funding that will help them with talent acquisition and further business development. Usually, with Series B funding, VCs that specialize in later-stage growth and development will invest, on average, $33 million.

Series C funding: By the time a company becomes eligible for Series C funding, they are already successful. In this stage, the company is simply seeking to develop new product lines or open up to new markets. Investors will most likely be private equity firms or hedge funds that have hundreds of millions in liquid capital at their disposal.

Series D funding or later: This is the funding right before a company goes public with an IPO. A company might take this funding to acquire smaller companies to help boost its revenue or customer/user numbers.* It's the "final push."

---

*TBF had a number of offers from companies, like internet brands, looking to purchase us to boost their revenue and users in the fashion/beauty space prior to going public.

How to Pitch

You've attracted the investor, you've got your materials, you're in the room . . . what now?

Well, first things first: know that this meeting can be in a variety of places. If you're dealing with an angel investor, you might be pitching to them out at a coffee shop. If they are a VC, you might be meeting with them in an office. Or maybe you meet a VC at a conference and they ask you to make a pitch *on the spot*.

The important thing is that you are prepared. As soon as you start looking for investors, you should know what your business plan is, what your marketing plan is, who your team is, why your product stands out from the competition, etc. If you outline this information *beforehand*, then you won't be caught off guard in the moment.

Elevator Pitch

As we saw in Step 3, an elevator pitch is a short description of your company, the problem you're trying to solve, and the size of the market. The idea is that if you were stuck on an elevator with your target investor you would be able to say all of this before the ride was over. Remember that short description of your company you did way back in Step 3? Well, guess what: this is also your elevator pitch.

The Pitch Deck

Generally, a pitch includes a slide presentation of all your hard-hitting points.

Guy Kawasaki, Silicon Valley venture capitalist, author, marketing specialist, and one of the Apple originals who popularized the term "evangelist" in marketing (really), coined the 10/20/30 rule for pitch decks. He says that a successful pitch will adhere to three rules:

1. **It has ten slides.** Why? Because despite our ability to binge-watch Netflix for seven hours straight, we do not have the capacity to pay attention to more meaningful content for more than ten slides.
2. **It takes twenty minutes.** You usually get one hour to have your meeting, so you want to make it count. There can be one person who has all the questions. Make your presentation no longer than twenty minutes so your hour in the room gives you enough time to get through the presentation and have a hearty discussion at the end of it without eating into anyone's lunch hour.
3. **The font is no smaller than thirty points.** No one wants to be straining to read the novel that you've packed onto your slide. If they try, instead of paying attention to your presentation, they'll be zeroed in on reading. Make your words the story and your slide the synopsis.

So what should be included in those ten slides?

Tool: Kawasaki's Ten Slides

Slide 1: The title. Duh. Your company name. Your name. Contact info. A cool nonintrusive logo if you've got one.

Slide 2: The problem the market faces that your unique product or service will help solve.

Slide 3: The value proposition. In other words, how does your product/service provide value to help resolve that problem or provide pleasure (or both!)?

> **Slide 4**: The underlying magic—What is your product? This is where you add a demo or a graphic explaining your product. If you can explain it in a graphic, it is worth so much more.
>
> **Slide 5**: The business model. By this point you know how to drive that train from investment to financial glory.
>
> **Slide 6**: Market plan. How are you going to reach people?
>
> **Slide 7**: Competitive analysis. How does the crowd look out there? How are you going to stand out?
>
> **Slide 8**: Management team. Everyone in your ether who is going to make said financial glory happen. It doesn't have to be perfect, it just has to be enough.
>
> **Slide 9**: Financial forecasting. Where will your business be three years from now? You got some good stats to back that up?
>
> **Slide 10**: Where are you now and how are you going to use the funds to get to where you want to go? What have you accomplished? How does what you've done speak to your ability to go where they, as investors, need you to go?

So a Venture Capitalist Wants to Invest, Now What?

So what comes after the decision? You get a term sheet.

What's a term sheet?

It's a nonbinding document that outlines the terms and conditions of an agreement between the investor and a business. It usually includes elements such as the amount of investment, equity percentage, degree of decision-making power, liquidation terms, anti-dilutive provisions, length of relationship, and the current company valuation. It is essentially a less formal letter of intent that spells out exactly what each party wants out of their relationship. It is the lead-up to a formal legally binding contract.

What many Builders don't know is that you can negotiate the terms and even the valuation listed in the term sheet. The key to negotiating effectively is to really understand your market and the valuations and investment amounts your competitors are receiving. If you know that a similar company is being valued at $5 million and an investor is valuing your company at $4 million, you are empowered to push back. Check online databases like Crunchbase or PitchBook (you can get a short-term free trial) to find out how much your competitors have raised. You can also search for details of their raise on sites like *TechCrunch* and *Business Insider*. As a venture capitalist, I actually expect to negotiate the term sheet. Good investors are open to hearing fact-based pushback from founders.

If you've made it to the point of a term sheet—congratulations! That is a huge deal. According to a Stanford study, out of one hundred startups actively considered, the average VC will meet with twenty-five, actively research about eight, and offer term sheets to one or two.

After everyone agrees to the term sheet and a lawyer draws up a formal contract—congratulations again! You've got yourself an investor.

So What's Your End Goal?

Let's say you've read through this entire step and you're still not sure which paths are right for you. Funding or no funding? Crowdfunding or VC?

Yes, I know, it's a lot to take in.

But let me remind you of an easy way to make any decision for your business (funding or otherwise): return to your core values.

A Final Note

While I do recommend preparedness when it comes to your funding needs for your business, this is not to say that you cannot change your goals to accommodate a changing industry or a changing you.

This is what I ran into when I was building The Budget Fashionista. Had I built the site today, I probably would have taken venture funding. The Budget Fashionista was revenue positive, with significant cash flow. I didn't need investment. Instead I got three small loans of about $15,000 apiece from Accion.

By the time venture did become available for content-based websites, and servers did become cheaper, and podcasts did start to become part of our everyday lives, I finally had interest from both VCs and private equity firms. And they were *great* offers. If they had come across my path five years earlier, when we were rapidly scaling and in need of more servers (this was before the cloud), it would have been perfect.

But, by that point, *I* had changed. I was making a lot of money that was 100 percent my money. I had built TBF for over ten years, and taking that money from the PEs or the VCs meant that I would have to stay because they wanted both the talent and the traffic. I would have had an "earn-out," a standard clause when a company is bought. An earn-out requires key staff to stay on the company after sale, sometimes for up to three years, to help with the transition to a new owner and ensure that the company can be successful once the founders leave. I didn't want TBF to be my whole life. I felt like I had made the impact I wanted to make. Hell, "fashionista" became common terminology outside New York in large part because of me. I was ready to move on.

So I said no and sold The Budget Fashionista instead.

Because I was 100 percent owner, that meant I got 100 percent of the proceeds. I remember going into my bank the day the wire for the sale cleared. The teller was a brother, and upon seeing the zeros in my bank account he said, "Girl, you are doing very well for yourself."

I am glad that I gave myself the option to move on. Now, with Genius Guild, I get to be a venture capitalist myself and invest in what I want to invest in.

I love that my trajectory turned out that way.

You got this.

We learned about gratitude and humility—that so many people had a hand in our success, from the teachers who inspired us to the janitors who kept our school clean . . . and we were taught to value everyone's contribution and treat everyone with respect.

Michelle Obama

EPILOGUE

Breathe. You Just Built the Damn Thing.

You've taken your initial idea and turned it into a fully functioning business. You built the damn thing. Congratulations! But hang on. That doesn't mean you can go and start acting entitled all of a sudden. Remember where you came from, Builder!

This isn't the end. Entrepreneurship is a lifelong endeavor. Keep learning, keep growing, keep challenging yourself, and, even in the face of MASSIVE success, remember to return to those core values that make you who you are.

One thing Builders often forget to do after climbing impossible mountains: take a moment to breathe and reflect.

It's deeply challenging to build a creative life as a member of communities where taking a pause conflicts with stereotypes about our identity that others—and maybe we ourselves—hold. Strong Black women. The smart Asian math nerd. The hardworking Latinx laborer. Remember that as the CEO of your company you are the center of the wheel. If you are broken, the wheel (your business) doesn't spin.

Taking a minute to reflect helps you to put things in perspective. Perspective is very useful when building a company because at times everything seems urgent, but not everything *is* urgent.

Remember what we've learned on our journey together. Start with getting your mind right. Remember the four P's of any great entrepreneur: Potential, Process, Performance, and Pivot. You want a solid foundation of knowledge to draw on and a good game plan, but you also need the ability to make changes on the fly. Pursuing a dream means you are going to experience failures, by definition. The important part is to keep moving forward ... with the right tools, like a mindfulness practice, a set of core values, a personal mission statement, a Strengths, Weaknesses, Opportunities, and Threats (SWOT) analysis, a personal advisory board, and a clear exit number.

Don't forget the golden rule: *a good business solves a problem.* Successful ones find solutions to problems many people have and are willing to pay for, and use the Build-Measure-Learn feedback loop. Once you've used this process to achieve product-market fit, it's time to put together your business model.

Note that no entrepreneur is an island (after all, business is about serving the needs of other people).

And remember that incubator program where I pitched my idea for a startup centered on ethnic hair products? And the Voldemort of Venture Capital, who said no one would ever invest in a beauty company run by a Black woman?

Well, the market has spoken, and it turns out people *do* care about the Black beauty industry. Hell, in 2021, even John Oliver, white dude of all white dudes, did an entire show on Black hair.

The Entitleds were wrong.

Stay humble, stay human, and Build the Damn Thing.

You GOT this ...

ACKNOWLEDGMENTS

When I started writing this book I thought it was going to be easy-peasy. I mean, this *is* my second book.

Let me tell you, writing a book is damn HARD. Full stop.

I thank God for constantly reminding me that the universe is conspiring for my greatness, even when sometimes I might fail to believe it. And for putting a truly amazing group of people in my life whose constant support, texts, and sometimes yells got me through this process.

I'm so lucky to have a visionary editor, Merry, and a great literary agent, Mackenzie, who've supported me as I wrote this book through a pandemic and a global uprising that started six blocks away from where I went to elementary school in Minneapolis. Also thank you to my researchers, Andy and Sarah, whose detailed work helped to make this book stronger.

I also want to thank the team at Genius Guild, who gave me the gift of grace during this process and supported me with an endless supply of brilliant memes and encouraging words. Building a business is damn hard. Full stop. You all make it worth it.

A big shout-out to my dearest friends and brothers, Sira and JB, who read many, many, many versions of this book and gave the most thorough feedback ever (with citations). Let me tell you it pays to have a university professor and an award-winning author as best friends/brothers.

And my family, who've been supportive of every crazy thing I've done

ACKNOWLEDGMENTS

since birth (and I've done some CRAZY.com things). Thank you, Tobias, Karen, Robert, Mariah, Trent, Tami, Papa Jay, Doonie, and Grandma Mary. A very special thank you to my Christian, whose Black boy joy fuels me every day. You've earned that dog.

Last but not least, thank you to my father, Robert Finney, whose vision for his life was so big that it allowed me to have an even bigger vision for my own.

NOTES

Prologue: A Builder's Story

xvi **who aren't white men:** "United States Population (LIVE)," *Worldometer*, https://www.worldometers.info/world-population/us-population.

xvii **"like Mark Zuckerberg":** Nathaniel Rich, "Silicon Valley's Start-Up Machine," *New York Times*, May 2, 2013, https://www.nytimes.com/2013/05/05/magazine/y-combinator-silicon-valleys-start-up-machine.html.

xviii **half a trillion dollars:** "Black Women: Statistics," Black Demographics, https://blackdemographics.com/population/black-women-statistics/; Tamara E. Holmes, "Feature: The Industry That Black Women Built," *Essence*, last updated December 6, 2020, https://www.essence.com/news/money-career/business-black-beauty/; Antonia Opiah, "The Changing Business of Black Hair, a Potentially $500b Industry," *HuffPost*, March 24, 2014, https://www.huffpost.com/entry/the-changing-business-of-_b_4650819.

Introduction: Getting Started: How to Build the Damn Thing

2 **clearly illustrates this point:** Adam Hayes, "Venture Capital," Investopedia, reviewed May 15, 2021, https://www.investopedia.com/terms/v/venturecapital.asp.

3 **"We look very hard":** Jessica Guynn, "Michael Moritz Taking Heat for Comments About Hiring Women," *USA Today*, December 3, 2015, https://www.usatoday.com/story/tech/2015/12/03/michael-moritz-sequoia-capital-women-diversity-silicon-valley/76736642.

6 **typical small business:** U.S. Small Business Administration, Office of Advocacy, https://cdn.advocacy.sba.gov/wp-content/uploads/2020/06/04144224/2020-Small-Business-Economic-Profile-US.pdf; Sean Peek, "How to Know If You Really Classify as a Small Business," *Business News Daily*, updated August 4, 2020, https://www.businessnewsdaily.com/295-sba-size-standards-small-business.html.

11 **1 billion Instagram accounts:** "Blog Statistics and Demographics," *Caslon Analytics Blogging*, February 2009, https://www.gwern.net/docs/technology/2009-arnold-bloggingstatisticsanddemographics.html#many; Prayiush, "Number of Blogs up from 35 Million in 2006 to 181 Million by the End of 2011," updated March 10, 2012, https://dazeinfo.com/2012/03/10/number-of-blogs-up-from-35-million-in-2006-to-181-million-by-the-end-of-2011; "Number of blogs worldwide from 2006 to 2011," Statista

NOTES

Research Department, March 12, 2012, https://www.statista.com/statistics/278527/number-of-blogs-worldwide/; "Cumulative total of Tumblr blogs from May 2011 to April 2020," Statista Research Department, January 27, 2021, https://www.statista.com/statistics/256235/total-cumulative-number-of-tumblr-blogs/; Jasmine Enberg, "Global Instagram Users 2020," *Insider Intelligence*, December 8, 2020, https://www.emarketer.com/content/global-instagram-users-2020.

11 *The Budget Fashionista* in August 2003: *The Budget Fashionista*, "I am looking for a good baby bag. Who makes them?," *The Budget Fashionista*, August 19, 2003; archived at Wayback Machine.

Step 1: Get Your Mind Right:
How to Build Your Internal Foundation

19 **leaders called TheLi.st:** "TheLi.st," New Power Media, https://www.theli.st.

19 **free month of a meditation app:** "LA County Is Stronger Together," *Headspace*, https://www.headspace.com/lacounty.

19 **"that is why I succeed":** "Michael Jordan," Forbes Quotes: Thoughts on the Business of Life, https://www.forbes.com/quotes/11194/.

23 **in impoverished communities:** "Our History," OIC of America, https://oicofamerica.org/our-history.

24 **rate was 11.5 percent:** "Schlitz Brewing Company," https://emke.uwm.edu/entry/schlitz-brewing-company/; "Unemployment Rate in Wisconsin (WIUR)," U.S. Bureau of Labor Statistics, retrieved from FRED, Federal Reserve Bank of St. Louis, https://fred.stlouisfed.org/series/WIUR.

26 **mortgage to fund your business:** Emily Moss, Kriston McIntosh, Wendy Edelberg, and Kristen Broady, "The Black-white wealth gap left Black households more vulnerable," Brookings, December 8, 2020, https://www.brookings.edu/blog/up-front/2020/12/08/the-black-white-wealth-gap-left-black-households-more-vulnerable.

26 **throughout Houston, Texas:** Girls Tyme, https://www.youtube.com/watch?v=Lf9_3-XSxSE; https://www.youtube.com/watch?v=c4QIdMjqmTo.

26 **neon green, and white:** Jill Hopkins and Joe DeCeault, "Beyoncé 2: Star Search," WBEZ Chicago, November 22, 2019, 12:01 a.m. CT, https://www.wbez.org/stories/beyonce-2-star-search/f5726004-c463-4d08-8384-4123efdb8b0d.

27 **to become a star:** Kelly Bertog, "My Worst Day: Beyoncé," December 16, 2019, https://kellybertog.medium.com/my-worst-day-beyonc%C3%A9-506d2a7fa82.

27 **most powerful women in media:** Alana Horowitz, "15 People Who Were Fired Before They Became Filthy Rich," *Business Insider*, April 25, 2011, https://www.businessinsider.com/15-people-who-were-fired-before-they-became-filthy-rich-2011-4#walt-disneys-newspaper-editor-told-the-aspiring-cartoonist-he-wasnt-creative-enough-1.

28 **her signature skills:** Associated Press, "Katelyn Ohashi wins 1st senior event," ESPN, March 2, 2013, https://www.espn.com/olympics/gymnastics/story/_/id/9007785/american-katelyn-ohashi-15-wins-first-senior-gymnastics-competition.

28 **Fremont Street Experience:** Vegas Experience, https://vegasexperience.com.

28 **at the Shipyard Bar:** Dave Trumbore, "Las Vegas Almost Built a Full Scale USS Enterprise from Star Trek," *Collider*, April 8, 2012, https://collider.com/star-trek-enterprise-vegas.

NOTES

30   **own public humiliation:** Gus Garcia-Roberts, "Hollywood producer Gary Goddard accused of sexual misconduct by 8 former child actors," *LA Times*, December 20, 2017, https://www.latimes.com/business/la-fi-ct-goddard-accusers-20171220-story.html.

30   **"Awasoruk Jam":** "Star Trek: The Experience," Wikipedia, https://en.wikipedia.org/wiki/Star_Trek:_The_Experience.

31   **and an okay photographer:** Keith Major Photography, https://www.keithmajor.com.

32   **the investment fund 10100:** Mike Isaac, "Uber's C.E.O. Plays with Fire," *New York Times*, April 23, 2017, https://www.nytimes.com/2017/04/23/technology/travis-kalanick-pushes-uber-and-himself-to-the-precipice.html; Steven Tweedie and Danielle Muoio, "Former Uber CEO Travis Kalanick sued by early investor Benchmark Capital over fraud allegations," *Business Insider*, August 10, 2017, https://www.businessinsider.com/uber-travis-kalanick-sued-for-alleged-fraud-by-benchmark-capital-2017-8; Sissi Cao, "Travis Kalanick Has a Plan for the $1.4B He Made Selling Uber Stock . . . Well, Sort of," *Observer*, March 8, 2018, https://observer.com/2018/03/travis-kalanick-launches-10100-vc-fund.

33   **Potential, Process, and Performance:** Thomas W. Y. Man, Theresa Lau, and K. F. Chan, "The Competitiveness of Small and Medium Enterprises: A Conceptualization with Focus on Entrepreneurial Competencies," *Journal of Business Venturing* 17 (2002): 123–42, https://wenku.baidu.com/view/a15a8c19c5da50e2524d7f11.html.

37   **to build a successful company:** Carol Dweck, "What Having a Growth Mindset Actually Means," *Harvard Business Review*, January 13, 2016, https://hbr.org/2016/01/what-having-a-growth-mindset-actually-means.

38   **Silicon Valley (Black population: 2.3 percent):** "New York City, New York Population 2021," World Population Review, https://worldpopulationreview.com/us-cities/new-york-city-ny-population; "Population Share by Race/Ethnicity: Santa Clara & San Mateo Counties," Silicon Valley Indicators, https://siliconvalleyindicators.org/data/people/talent-flows-diversity/racial-and-ethnic-composition/population-share-by-race-ethnicity.

42   **startup founder is forty-five:** Pierre Azoulay, Benjamin F. Jones, J. Daniel Kim, and Javier Miranda, "Research: The Average Age of a Successful Startup Founder is 45," *Harvard Business Review*, July 2018, https://hbr.org/2018/07/research-the-average-age-of-a-successful-startup-founder-is-45.

42   **for $1.6 billion:** Lucinda Shen, "Back from the dead, Brandless moves into the creator economy and e-commerce rollups," *Fortune*, August 5, 2021, https://fortune.com/2021/08/05/back-from-the-dead-brandless-moves-into-the-creator-economy-and-e-commerce-rollups/; Kaarin Vembar, "Brandless raises $118M in funding round," *Retail Dive*, August 5, 2021, https://www.retaildive.com/news/brandless-raises-118m-in-funding-round/604518/; Brandless, https://brandless.com.

43   **University of Houston:** Paige Leskin, "These 23 successful tech moguls never graduated college," *Insider*, May 26, 2019, https://www.businessinsider.com/mark-zuckerberg-steve-jobs-tech-executives-never-graduated-college-dropouts-2019-5#matt-mullenweg-founder-wordpress-2.

48   **American Intellectual Property Law Association:** Chris Neumeyer, "Managing Costs of Patent Litigation," *IPWatchdog*, February 5, 2013, http://www.ipwatchdog.com/2013/02/05/managing-costs-of-patent-litigation/id=34808.

NOTES

Step 2: Your Personal Success Toolbox: How to Gather the Tools to Build Your Company

52 **of a mindfulness practice:** Lauren Effron, "Michael Jordan, Kobe Bryant's Meditation Coach on How to Be 'Flow Ready' and Get in the Zone," ABC News, April 6, 2016, https://abcnews.go.com/Health/michael-jordan-kobe-bryants-meditation-coach-flow-ready/story?id=38175801.

52 **her powerhouse serves:** "How Proper Breathing Helps Your Tennis," Feel Tennis, April 24, 2021, https://www.feeltennis.net/breathing-in-tennis.

53 **he walked away:** Emily Yahr, "Dave Chappelle gets real: Does he regret walking away from millions of dollars?," *Washington Post*, June 11, 2014, https://www.washingtonpost.com/news/arts-and-entertainment/wp/2014/06/11/dave-chappelle-gets-real-does-he-regret-walking-away-from-millions-of-dollars/; Pamela Engel, "Why Dave Chappelle Walked Away from $50 Million," *DC Nitelife*, https://dcnitelife.com/dave-chappelle-walked-away-50-million.

53 **seat at the table:** E. Alex Jung, "Michaela the Destroyer," *Vulture*, July 6, 2020, https://www.vulture.com/article/michaela-coel-i-may-destroy-you.html.

58 **highly than others rate them:** Rakesh Kochhar and Anthony Cilluffo, "How Wealth Inequality Has Changed in the U.S. Since the Great Recession, by Race, Ethnicity and Income," Pew Research, November 1, 2017, https://www.pewresearch.org/fact-tank/2017/11/01/how-wealth-inequality-has-changed-in-the-u-s-since-the-great-recession-by-race-ethnicity-and-income.

63 **financial suicide:** David Dunning, Chip Heath, and Jerry M. Suls, "Flawed Self-Assessment: Implications for Health, Education, and the Workplace," *Psychological Science in the Public Interest* 5, no. 3 (2004): 69–106, https://psycnet.apa.org/record/2005-09490-002.

64 **a few extras:** Dr. Saul McLeod, "Maslow's Hierarchy of Needs," *Simply Psychology*, December 29, 2020, https://www.simplypsychology.org/maslow.html.

Step 3: You're NOT Your Customer: How to Make Sure Your Business Solves a Problem

68 **its first five weeks:** "Operating System Interface Design Between 1981–2009," *Web Designer Depot*, March 11, 2009, https://www.webdesignerdepot.com/2009/03/operating-system-interface-design-between-1981-2009; Alex Soojung-Kim Pang, "The Xerox PARC Visit," Making the Macintosh: Technology and Culture in Silicon Valley, October 16, 2021, https://web.stanford.edu/dept/SUL/sites/mac/parc.html; William A. Sherden, *Best Laid Plans* (Santa Barbara, CA: ABC-CLIO, 2011), 68; Alyssa Newcomb, "Why Windows 95 Was a Game-Changer for Computer Users Everywhere," ABC News, August 24, 2015, https://abcnews.go.com/Technology/windows-95-game-changer-computer-users/story?id=33212036.

75 **losses for Black homeowners:** Jill Sheridan, "A Black Woman Says She Had to Hide Her Race to Get a Fair Home Appraisal," NPR, May 21, 2021, https://www.npr.org/2021/05/21/998536881/a-black-woman-says-she-had-to-hide-her-race-to-get-a-fair-home-appraisal.

76 **$5 billion to the U.S. economy:** "Industry Overview," Coin Laundry Association, https://www.coinlaundry.org/for-investors/industry-overview.

NOTES

77 **menstruating each day:** Erica Sánchez and Leah Rodriguez, "Period Poverty: Everything You Need to Know," Global Citizen, February 5, 2019, https://www.globalcitizen.org/en/content/period-poverty-everything-you-need-to-know/?template=next.

77 **213 million small businesses:** D. Clark, "Number of SMEs Worldwide 2000–2020," Statista, September 30, 2021, https://www.statista.com/statistics/1261592/global-smes/.

77 **59 million people:** "2018 Small Business Profile," U.S. Small Business Administration, Office of Advocacy, https://www.sba.gov/sites/default/files/advocacy/2018-Small-Business-Profiles-US.pdf.

80 **and create discomfort:** Emma Goldberg, "Many Lack Access to Pads and Tampons. What Are Lawmakers Doing About It?," *New York Times*, January 13, 2021, https://www.nytimes.com/2021/01/13/us/tampons-pads-period.html; Allison Sadlier, "New Research Reveals How Much the Average Woman Spends per Month on Menstrual Products," *SWNS Digital*, November 27, 2019, https://swnsdigital.com/2019/11/new-research-reveals-how-much-the-average-woman-spends-per-month-on-menstrual-products/#:~:text=Results%20revealed%20the%20average%20woman,(ages%2012%2D52).

80 **$5 billion per year:** "Key Statistics Laundromat Investors Should Know," Martin Ray Laundry Systems, https://martinray.com/p-33942-key-statistics-laundromat-investors-should-know.html; John Egan, "The 8 Places Where People Spend Too Much Time at the Laundromat," *The Laundry Bag*, http://www.presscleaners.com/blog/the-8-places-where-people-spend-too-much-time-at-the-laundromat.

80 **focus on scaling their businesses:** "2018 Small Business Profile," U.S. Small Business Administration, https://www.sba.gov/sites/default/files/advocacy/2018-Small-Business-Profiles-US.pdf; "Payroll Stats for Small Businesses," Zenefits.com, https://www.zenefits.com/workest/payroll-stats-small-business.

80 **4.5 billion tacos every day:** "Fun Facts About Tacos That You Probably Never Knew," *Borracha*, https://borrachavegas.com/fun-facts-tacos; National Taco Day, https://www.nationaltacoday.com.

Step 4: Product-Market Fit: How to Turn Your Solution into a Money-Making Business

87 **valued at close to $1 billion:** Keisha Morant, "Is the First Black-Owned Tech Unicorn Finally Within Reach?," POCIT, https://peopleofcolorintech.com/front/is-the-first-black-tech-unicorn-within-reach/; "10 Barbershop Marketing Ideas. How to Promote Your Barbershop," Appointfix, July 8, 2021, https://www.appointfix.com/blog/barbershop-marketing-ideas.html; Yoonkee Sull, Sruthi Ramaswami, and Will Griffith, "Behind the Cuts: Squire, Powering the Barbershop Community," ICONIQ Growth, https://medium.com/iconiq-growth/behind-the-cuts-squire-powering-the-barbershop-community-81ca532dcd77; Derek Major, "Squire Barbershop Tech Founders Announce Funding Round of $60 Million, Tripling Valuation," *Black Enterprise*, August 5, 2021, https://www.blackenterprise.com/squire-barbershop-tech-founders-announce-funding-round-of-60-million-tripling-valuation/?test=prebid.

99 **the Amazon of shoes was born:** Ben Parr, "Breaking: Amazon Acquires Zappos for $850 Million," *Mashable*, July 22, 2009, https://mashable.com/archive/amazon-buys-zappos.

101 **above 2 percent is considered great:** Mark Irvine, "Facebook Ad Benchmarks for YOUR Industry [2019]," *WordStream*, updated October 12, 2021, https://www.word

NOTES

stream.com/blog/ws/2019/11/12/facebook-ad-benchmarks; Alisha Rechberg, "What Is a Good CTR for Google Ads?," Your Marketing People, August 5, 2021, https://your marketingpeople.com/blog/what-is-a-good-ctr-for-google-ads.

112 **Alexander Osterwalder in 2005:** "Business Model Design and Innovation," November 5, 2005, https://web.archive.org/web/20061213141941/http://business-model-design.blogspot.com/2005/11/what-is-business-model.html; "The Business Model Canvas," Strategyzer, n.d., https://www.strategyzer.com/canvas/business-model-canvas.

116 **global hair extension brand:** Susan Adams, "Long on Hair: The World's First Venture-Backed Human-Hair-Extension Company Wants to Be the Airbnb of Salons," *Forbes*, September 27, 2019, https://www.forbes.com/sites/susanadams/2019/09/27/long-on-hair-the-worlds-first-venture-backed-human-hair-extension-company-wants-to-be-the-airbnb-of-salons/?sh=68d9fc7173a3; Keisha Morant, "Is the First Black-Owned Tech Unicorn Finally Within Reach?," POCIT, https://peopleofcolorintech.com/front/is-the-first-black-tech-unicorn-within-reach/; "Mayvenn," PitchBook, https://pitchbook.com/profiles/company/56962-18#funding.

116 **over fifty thousand stylists:** Tamara E. Holmes, "Feature: The Industry That Black Women Built," *Essence*, October 22, 2019, https://www.essence.com/news/money-career/business-black-beauty/; Susan Adams, "Long on Hair: The World's First Venture-Backed Human-Hair-Extension Company Wants to Be the Airbnb of Salons," *Forbes*, September 27, 2019, https://www.forbes.com/sites/susanadams/2019/09/27/long-on-hair-the-worlds-first-venture-backed-human-hair-extension-company-wants-to-be-the-airbnb-of-salons/?sh=68d9fc7173a3.

Step 5: Squad Goals: How to Build an Amazing Team

132 **startups fail because of it:** Bryce Conlan, "Harvard Business School Professor Says 65% of Startups Fail for One Reason. Here's How to Avoid It," *Entrepreneur*, June 8, 2021, https://www.entrepreneur.com/article/370367.

150 **to make in a day:** Michael Lewis, "Obama's Way," *Vanity Fair*, https://www.vanityfair.com/news/2012/10/michael-lewis-profile-barack-obama.

157 **"it mattered the most":** John Doerr, *Measure What Matters* (New York: Portfolio/Penguin, 2018).

Step 6: Getting the Bag: How to Get the $$$ You Need to Grow Your Company

168 **credit cards (10.3 percent):** Tiffany Howard, "The State of Black Entrepreneurship in America," Center for Policy Analysis and Research, April 2019, https://www.cbcfinc.org/wp-content/uploads/2019/05/CPAR-Report-Black-Entrepreneurship-in-America.pdf.

168 **more than $1 million in outside venture funding:** "Women of Color in the United States," Catalyst, February 1, 2021, https://www.catalyst.org/research/women-of-color-in-the-united-states/; "Volume of VC Funding Raised by Black and Latina Women-Led Companies from 2018 to 2019," Statista, https://www.statista.com/statistics/1223143/venture-capital-funding-black-latina-women-led-startups/; Emma Hinchliffe, "The Number of Black Female Founders Who Have Raised More Than $1 Million Has Nearly Tripled Since 2018," *Fortune*, December 2, 2020, https://fortune.com/2020/12/02/black-women-female-founders-venture-capital-funding-vc-2020-project-diane/; "Project-

NOTES

Diane 2020: The State of Black & Latinx Women Founders," digitalundivided, https://www.digitalundivided.com/reports/projectdiane-2020.

168 **all women-led startups:** "Fuelling Better, More Diverse Ideas," State of European Tech 21, undated, https://stateofeuropeantech.com/chapter/better-ideas-better-companies/article/fuelling-better-more-diverse-ideas/.

171 **interviewed me about Genius Guild:** Rebecca Szkutak, "Kathryn Finney's Genius Guild Emerges from Stealth with $5 Million to Support Black Entrepreneurs," *Forbes*, April 6, 2021, https://www.forbes.com/sites/rebeccaszkutak/2021/04/05/kathryn-finneys-genius-guild-emerges-from-stealth-with-5-million-to-support-black-entrepreneurs/?sh=382b8a2424aa.

179 **have to pay it back:** Justin Song, "Average Small Business Loan Interest Rates in 2021: Comparing Top Lenders," ValuePenguin, updated March 15, 2021, https://www.valuepenguin.com/average-small-business-loan-interest-rates.

181 **that very high balance:** Rosemary Carlson, "Using a Credit Card to Finance Your Small Business," *The Balance*, updated on May 10, 2021, https://www.thebalancesmb.com/credit-cards-finance-business-393140.

186 **in the U.S. banking system:** Li Zhou, "The Paycheck Protection Program Failed Many Black-Owned Businesses," *Vox*, October 5, 2020, https://www.vox.com/2020/10/5/21427881/paycheck-protection-program-black-owned-businesses.

187 **$50,000 in microinvestment grants:** "2020 Investment Grants," The Doonie Fund, https://www.thedoonie.fund.

188 **interest rates are nationwide:** Justin Song, "Average Small Business Loan Interest Rates in 2021: Comparing Top Lenders," ValuePenguin, updated March 15, 2021, https://www.valuepenguin.com/average-small-business-loan-interest-rates.

188 **for a business loan:** Steve Nicastro and Jackie Veling, "5 Steps to Getting a Business Loan," Nerdwallet, September 2, 2021, https://www.nerdwallet.com/article/small-business/how-to-get-a-small-business-loan,

189 **average microloan is about $13,000:** Benjamin Pimentel, "6 Startup Business Loan Options for Entrepreneurs," Nerdwallet, August 23, 2021, https://www.nerdwallet.com/article/small-business/startup-business-loans.

197 **in the first forty-eight hours:** Stats, Kickstarter, https://www.kickstarter.com/help/stats.

201 **and fewer disclosure requirements:** "What Is the JOBS Act?," *Crowdfund Insider*, https://www.crowdfundinsider.com/what-is-the-jobs-act/; "Regulation Crowdfunding," Securities and Exchange Commission, March 17, 2021, https://www.sec.gov/smallbusiness/exemptofferings/regcrowdfunding.

203 **than projects without (30 percent):** Jayson Duncan, "How to Create a Video for Kickstarter," Miller Farm Media, September 23, 2013, https://millerfarmmedia.com/how-to-create-a-video-for-kickstarter/.

205 **75 percent of VC investments fail:** Deborah Gage, "The Venture Capital Secret: 3 Out of 4 Start-Ups Fail," *Wall Street Journal*, September 20, 2012, https://www.wsj.com/articles/SB10000872396390443720204578004980476429190.

213 **that same year, Nasty Gal filed:** Samantha Sharf, "What Sophia Amoruso Learned from Nasty Gal's Bankruptcy," *Forbes*, October 3, 2017, https://www.forbes.com/sites/samanthasharf/2017/10/03/what-sophia-amoruso-learned-from-nasty-gals-bankruptcy/?sh=6bb1b3464523.

NOTES

214 **sample the Nasty Gal style in person:** Sophia Amoruso, "Why I Raised Venture Capital Again," Girlboss, December 13, 2017, https://www.girlboss.com/read/sophia-amoruso-girlboss-seed-funding; Anna Merlan, "'Everything Really Hit Rock Bottom': How Nasty Gal's Culture Went Nasty," *Jezebel*, June 17, 2015, https://jezebel.com/everything-really-hit-rock-bottom-how-nasty-gals-cultu-1711454805; Shan Li, "Nasty Gal, Once a Fashion World Darling, Is Now Bankrupt. What Went Wrong?," *Los Angeles Times*, February 24, 2017, https://www.latimes.com/business/la-fi-nasty-gal-20170224-story.html.

215 **and build brand loyalty:** Alex Wilhelm, "Will ride-hailing profits ever come?," *TechCrunch*, February 12, 2021, https://techcrunch.com/2021/02/12/will-ride-hailing-profits-ever-come.

215 **"too complex too fast":** Sissi Cao, "A Conversation with Sophia Amoruso, the 'Girlboss' Founder of Nasty Gal," *Observer*, October 2, 2018, https://observer.com/2018/10/sophia-amoruso-girlboss-nasty-gal.

215 **encouraged unsustainable growth:** Sramana Mitra, "How Overfunding Killed Nasty Gal," *Inc.*, n.d., https://www.inc.com/linkedin/sramana-mitra/death-overfunding-nasty-gal-sramana-mitra.html.

217 **on average, $33 million:** Purity Muriuki, "Different Startup Growth Stages and What They Mean for Investors," *Startup Info*, June 14, 2021, https://startup.info/different-startup-growth-stages-and-what-they-mean-for-investors.

220 **need you to go:** Guy Kawasaki, "The Only 10 Slides You Need in Your Pitch," March 5, 2015, https://guykawasaki.com/the-only-10-slides-you-need-in-your-pitch.

221 **offer term sheets to one or two:** Paul Gompers, William Gornall, Steven N. Kaplan, and Ilya A. Strebulaev, "How Do Venture Capitalists Make Decisions?," Stanford University Graduate School of Business Research Paper No. 16-33, European Corporate Governance Institute (ECGI), Finance Working Paper No. 477/2016, June 29, 2016, revised May 10, 2017, https://papers.ssrn.com/sol3/papers.cfm?abstract_id=2801385.

Epilogue: Breathe. You Just Built the Damn Thing.

224 **"treat everyone with respect":** "Michelle Obama's Convention Speech," NPR, September 4, 2012, https://www.npr.org/2012/09/04/160578836/transcript-michelle-obamas-convention-speech.

INDEX

Note: Italicized page numbers indicate material in tables or illustrations.

abundance mindset, *138*, 141–42
Accion, 189, 222
accountants, 154
active listening, *139*
ad-based business model, *115*
advice. *See* lies told to Builders
advisory board, personal, 60–62, 129, 182
age of founders, average, 42
agile, staying, *139*, 156–57
Airtable, 39*n*
Amazon, *46*
angel investors, 168, *180*, 203–4
anger, xx, xxi
apparel companies, 214–15
Apple, *43*, 68
Away, *46*

Bad Boy, 6, *43*
bag. *See* funding
banks
  loans from, 168, *179*, 187–88
  and racial inequities, 186
barbershop booking app, 85–87
Berry, Halle, 19
Beyoncé, 26–27, 27*n*
Bighit Music, 45, 45*n*
BIG Incubator Program (BIG), 121
Black hair care/beauty industry
  author's idea pitched at incubator, xviii–xix, 45, 226
Black people/community
  and BIG Incubator Program, 121
  and digitalundivided's vision, 91
  and Doonie Fund, 187
  and funding sources, 119, 168
  and lack of diversity in startup world, 118–20, 194, 194*n*
  and median net worth, 25, 63
  and Paycheck Protection Program, 186
  pressure to be the best, xix
  and stereotypes, 225
BlogHer, 89–91, 90*n*, 92
blogs and bloggers
  growth of, *9–10*
  See also *The Budget Fashionista*
board of directors/advisors, personal, 60–62, 129, 182
bravery, practicing, *138*
breathwork, 52–53
brilliance/genius, daily practice of, *138*
BS meter, personal advisors with, 61–62
BTS (Bangtan Boys), xxvi, 45*n*
The Budget Fashionista (*TBF*)
  author's creation of, 9–13, 32
  funding offers/options, 217*n*, 222
  growth of, 9, 12–13
  sale of, 4, 13, 167–68, 222–23
  success of, xv, xxii
Builders
  challenges faced by, 1–2
  educational backgrounds of, 15
  and expectations for failure, 20
  internal foundation of (*see* mindset)
  leadership skills for, 124–26
  necessity of being twice as good, 4–5

INDEX

Builders (*cont.*)
   personal skill sets of (*see* toolbox for personal success)
   pressure to succeed, 25–26
   value of executive coaches for, 154–55
   See also entrepreneurship
Build-Measure-Learn (B-M-L) loop
   about, 84–85
   Build phase, 87–99
   Feedback phase, 99–108
   Learn phase, 109–10
   limiting investments in, 87, 95, 96–98
   repeating, 84*n*, 111
   See also Minimal Viable Products (MVP)
Business Insider, 221
business models
   about, 115–16
   and Business Model Canvas, 111–14, 112*n*
   eight popular, *114–15*
business plans, *7*, 112

capital table, 210
check-ins, daily, 159–60
chief of staff (COS), 150
chief operating officers (COO), 150
Clare, *46*
clarity, 55
Cocofloss, *46*
coding skills, 39–42
co-founders
   breakups with, 134
   building relationship with, 133–35
   with coding skills, 41
   founders compared to, *130–31*
   with industry expertise, 35
   outlining responsibilities of, 133–34
   pros/cons of adding, 131–32
   role of, *131*
   time spent together, 134–35
college background as common ground, 192
commitment as core value, *140*
communication
   and Business Model Canvas, 113
   and co-founders, 133
   and daily check-ins, 159–60
   and difficult conversations, 160, 160*n*
   and internal conflicts, 132
   over Zoom, 160
   staying agile with, 156–57

community, balancing needs of customers against, 109–10
competition, protecting your ideas from, 47–48
conferences, gathering feedback at, *105*
conflict, reducing unnecessary, 132, 146
consultants, 145, 146–47
consumer, personal experience as, 34–35
content sites, MVPs for, *89*
core values
   and employees/team, 136–43
   and funding options, 172–73, 221
   identifying company's values, 136–43
   identifying personal values, 53–56
   and leadership skills, 124, 125
   and personal mission statement, 57
costs of startups, *7*, 114
covering, xix (*note*)
COVID-19 pandemic
   and digital communication, 160
   and flexibility prioritized by employees, 145
   and origins of Genius Guild, 32
credit cards
   in early stages of building, 168, 180
   high costs associated with, 187
   pros/cons of, *179*, 181
crowdfunding, 193–203
   choosing a platform for, 199–201
   conversion rates for, 199
   democratizing effects of, 14
   draft email for, 197–98
   equity and non-equity based, 168
   fees associated with, 200–201
   and regulatory limits, 201
   as resource for Builders, 15
   setting a goal for campaign, 202
   timing of targeted list vs. general mailing list, 198–99
   videos for, 203
crowdinvesting, 193, 194
Crunchbase, 118, 194*n*, 221
CT Corporation, 154
customers
   balancing community with, 109–10
   customer discovery, 14
   focusing on needs of, 78
   identifying, in Business Model Canvas, 113
   prioritizing the experience of, 36–37

INDEX

data room/doc room, 209–11
decision-making, core values as a tool of, 140
delegation, importance of, 149
desktop interface in computing, 68–69
digitalundivided
  business model of, 116–17
  early funding for, 93–94
  FOCUS100 conference, 91, 92, 94, 106–7, 117, 118
  impact of, xxii
  Minimal Viable Products for, 89–94
  origins of, 32, 91
  pitch deck for, 93
  and product-market fit, 92, 121
  and ProjectDiane, 121
  vision of, 91
discovery process, 86
disintermediation business model, *115*
diversity, equity, and inclusion (DEI) budgets, 106
diversity in startup industry, lack of, 118–20, 194, 194*n*
Doonie Fund, 185, 186–87
dreams, clarity on, 55

E-commerce business model, *115*
Economist archetype, 151–52
educational backgrounds of founders, 15, 41–42, *43*
elevator pitches
  about, xviii (*note*)
  drafting, 79–80
  for venture capital, 218
empathy, 55
employees
  consultants, 135, 145, 146–47
  and core values, 136–43
  cost of hiring, 152–53
  and crowdfunding efforts, 202
  and employment law, 145*n*, 146
  equity for, 176
  firing/offboarding, 161–63
  friends/family as, 127–29, 163, 163*n*
  guidelines for hiring, 143–47
  incentivizing, 145
  and independent contractors, 146
  trial periods with, 144, 144*n*
  and true callings, 161–62
  trusting your instincts on, 146, 147

  when to bring in outside help, 135
  See also teams
employment of Builders
  checking agreements/contracts with, 63*n*
  and finding your exit number, 63–64
  resources available at place of, 63
Entitleds
  ability to leverage funding, 14, 164
  advantages enjoyed by, 1–2, 4–5
  information sharing habits of, 38
  lies told to Builders, 38–48
  narratives about Builders, 2–3
  risk-taking as a privilege of, 25
entrepreneurship
  of Black/Latinx women, 89, 106, 108, 117, 118–21, 186–87
  and growth mindset, 37
  as lifelong endeavor, 225
  as means to wealth creation, 9
  preparation as key to, 33
  and product-market fit, 83
  risks associated with, 18
  and self-care, 19
  video game analogy for, 1–2
  See also Builders; funding
ethnic hair care. *See* Black hair care/beauty industry
Etsy, 38
executive coaches, 154–55
exit number
  and budget for MVP, 87
  determining your, 63–64
  and funding options, 181
  and knowing when to walk away, 126

Facebook, 6, 210*n*
Facebook Ads, 101
fact-checking, importance of, 38
failure
  defying expectations for, 20, 21–22, 24
  as fate of most new companies, 18
  fear of, 19–20, 28–30, 31, 37
  and future success, 32
  getting comfortable with, 26
  and growth mindset, 27
  lessons gained from, 26, 27–28
  as part of the journey, 20, 25–33, 226
  and permission to fail, 24, 31–32
  as pivot opportunity, 37

INDEX

failure (*cont.*)
    and pressure to succeed, 25
    value of embracing, 32–33
families
    employment of family members, 127–29
    firing family members, 163, 163*n*
    funding from, 168, *178*, 182
    non-financial support from, 182–84
    seeking advice/feedback from, 78–79
family business
    and familial relationships, 127, 128
    lessons gained from, 70–71
    and repeating customers, 76
    and risk tolerance of co-founders, 132
Fast Company, 194*n*
fears
    facing your, 31
    of failure, 19–20, 28–30, 31, 37
    and fearlessness as core value, 55–56
    reducing, through preparation, 33
feedback
    implementing, 109–10
    and market research, 109
    on Minimal Viable Products, 99–103, *104–5*
    negative, 108
    soliciting honest, 100–103
    sources of, *104–5*
financing. *See* funding
firing employees, 161–63
fixed mindsets, 37
Floyd, George, 32, 108, 168
Forbes magazine, 171–72
Ford Motor Company, 83
foundations offering grants, 185
founders
    average age of, 42
    co-founders compared to, *130–31* (see also co-founders)
    educational backgrounds of, 15, 41–42, *43*
    ingredients of great, 33–38
    lack of diversity in, 118–20, 194, 194*n*
    leadership skills for, 124–26
    and pattern-matching bias, xvii
    role of, *130*
    See also Builders; entrepreneurship
freemium business model, *115*
friends
    as employees, 127, 163, 163*n*
    funding from, 182
    non-financial support from, 182–84
    seeking advice/feedback from, 78–79
funding, 167–223
    angel investors, 168, *180*, 203–4
    bank loans, 168, *179*, 187–88
    for building MVP, 170
    and business models, 116
    and co-founders, 131
    and core values, 172–73, 221
    credit cards, 168, *179*, 180, 181, 187
    crowdfunding, 14, 15, 168, *179*, 193–203
    crowdinvesting, 193, 194
    Doonie Fund, 185, 186–87
    Entitleds' ability to leverage, 14, 164
    equity-based, 168, 169–70, 177, *179–80*, 203–4
    and ethnic minority startups, 119, 168
    to exploit rare opportunities, 170
    from family/friends, 168, *178*, 182–84
    grants, 170, *178*, 184–87
    high costs of some options, 171, 212–13
    and lawyers, 153
    and limiting personal investments, 87
    microloans, 189
    nondilutive, 14
    non-equity-based, 168–69, 177, *178–79*
    owning your choices for, 171–72, 208
    personal savings, 168–69, *178*, 180–81
    and product-market fit, 170, 175–76
    questions to ask regarding, 172–76
    resources for, 15, 15*n*
    risks associated with, 168–69
    for scaling a company, 164, 169, 170, 206, 217
    and small businesses compared to startups, 7
    understanding how you will use, 174–75
    understanding your need for, 173–74
    when to take money, 169–72
    See also venture capital/capitalists

gender of founders, 118
Genius Guild
    about, xxii
    and buy-in from support system, 130
    company values of, 136–43
    and domain experience of author, 34
    feedback sought for, 108
    fifteen-minute check-ins at, 159
    and funding offers/sources, 171–72, 190

INDEX

Greenhouse Fund of, 140, 142, 204
idea behind, 46
and Objectives and Key Results framework, 157–58
origins of, 32
search for lawyer for, 153
sense of community in, 125
and staying agile, 156
giveaways, budgeting for, 103
Glossier, 45, *46*
goals
   clarity on, 55
   and Objectives and Key Results framework, 157–59
   of startups vs. small businesses, *7*
GoFundMe, 193
Google Ads, 101
Google Analytics, 95, 95*n*
Google Trends, 74
government grants for businesses, 184–85
grants, 170, *178*, 184–87
graphical user interface (GUI) in computing, 68–69
Greenhouse Fund of Genius Guild, 140, 142, 204
Groupon, 37
growth, commitment to, *140*
growth mindset, 27, 37–38
Gusto, *46*

hair care industry. *See* Black hair care/beauty industry
Hale, Kathryn "Doonie," 186–87
health, prioritizing, 124–25
High Output Management (Grove), 157
hobbies, businesses vs., 69, 69*n*, 77, 106
homeownership, 75
honesty and trust, *139*
Horowitz, Ben, 116
human resources, outsourced, 77, 80
Hurley, Chad, *43*
Huston, Therese, 160*n*

ideas, 67–81
   defining pain points in, 73
   and drafting an elevator pitch, 79–80
   examples of, 76–80
   finding the scale of the problem, 73–74
   four steps to defining, 71–78
   in search of a problem, 69–70, 77

soliciting honest feedback on, 100–103
that customers will pay for, 69, 72, 74–75
that draw repeatable customers, 72, 75–76
that solve problems, 71–72
Imira, Diishan, 116
incubator program from hell, xv–xxii, 226
independent contractors, 146
initial public offerings (IPO), 6
insecurity, 37, 59
Inside the Actors Studio, 53
Instacart, *46*
instincts, trusting, 146, 147
insurance costs, 152
integrity, 53–55
intellectual property, protecting, 47–48
intentions, clarity on, 55
interest groups, offline, *104*
IPSY, 45

Jaffe, Stanley, 29–30, 30*n*
Jemison, Mae, 28*n*
Jobs, Steve, 42, *43*, 68
Jones, Darlene Gillard, 94, 94*n*, 134–35
Jordan, Michael, 19, 27, 52
joy, prioritizing, 125

Kabbage, 38
Kawasaki, Guy, 218–19
key results framework, 157–59
Kickstarter, 120, 193, 197, 200
knowledge, two types of, 34–35
Knowles, Mathew, 27

Lansing, Sherry, 29
LaRon, Songe, 85–87
The Last Dance (ESPN series), 52
LastSwab, *46*
Las Vegas, *Star Trek* construction project in, 28–30
Latinx community
   and BIG Incubator Program, 121
   and digitalundivided's vision, 91
   and funding sources, 168
   pressure to be the best, xix
   and stereotypes, 225
laughter, importance of, 62
lawyers, 153, 207, 207*n*
leadership skills, 124–26
The Lean Startup (Ries), 84, 84*n*

INDEX

Lean Startup Methodology (LSM), 121
learning, prioritizing, 125, 150–51, 225
legacies, xxiii, 118–21
Lemonade, 46
Lenihan, Lawrence, 215
lies told to Builders, 38–48
  on building a certain type of startup, 45–47
  on following the "rules," 44–45
  on importance of coding skills, 39–42
  on importance of elite education, 41–42, 43
  on protecting your idea from thieves, 47–48
LinkedIn, 190
TheLi.st, 19
listeners, personal advisors as, 62
listening, active, *139*
Lizzo, xiii
LOLA, *46*

Mailchimp, 199
mall, gathering feedback at, *105*
Man, Thomas W. Y., 33
mantras, 52–53
market-based economy, 67, 75
marketplace business model, *114*
market research, 109
Maslow's Hierarchy of Needs, 64*n*, 76
Measure What Matters (Doerr), 159*n*
median net worth, racial disparities in, 25, 63
meetings, goal of getting to the next, 5
meetups, local, *104*
mental health, spending time on, 19, 125
meritocracy, xvii, 2
Method Man, 165
microinvestment grants, 187
microloans, 185, 189, 222
Microsoft Windows, 68
Milwaukee, Wisconsin, 20–23
mindfulness, 52–53, *139*
mindset, 17–48
  critical importance of, 18–19, 226
  and defying expectations, 20–25
  and fear of failure, 19–20
  getting comfortable with failure and risk, 25–33
  and importance of self-care, 17–18
  and ingredients of great founders, 33–38
  and perspectives on success, 18–19

  and self-care, 19
  See also lies told to Builders; toolbox for personal success
Minimal Viable Products (MVP)
  about, 84
  and course corrections/pivots, 98
  early sketches of, 93
  and familial support system, 127
  first steps, per business type, *89*
  implementing feedback, 109–10
  measuring results from, 99–108
  minimizing investments in, 87, 95, 96–98
  Taco Truck (example), 94–96, *95*
  taking funding to build, 170
  under-$100 success stories, 99
  See also Build-Measure-Learn (B-M-L) loop
Minneapolis, Minnesota, 24
mission statement, personal, 57
mistakes made by leaders, 143
mitú, 42, *43*
motivation, 59, 62
Mullenweg, Matt, 12*n*, *43*

Nash, Diane, 119–20
Nasty Gal, 213–16
negative work habits, 59
networks
  and crowdfunding, 194–95, 196–97
  identifying, 59
New York startup community, xv–xxii
Nichols, Nichelle, 28, 28*n*
nondilutive funding, 14, 14*n*
nongovernmental organizations (NGOs), 185
nonprofit business grants, 185

Obama, Barack, 150*n*, 201
Obama, Michelle, 224
Objectives and Key Results (OKRs) framework, 157–59, 159*n*
on-demand business model, *114*
openness, maintaining, *139*
opportunities, identifying, 58, 59
Opportunities Industrialization Center (OIC), 23, 24

pain points, identifying, 72
Paramount Studios, 29
pattern-matching bias, xvi–xvii, xx, 41
payroll processors, 77, 154*n*

INDEX

perfection, 31, 36
performance (execution), 36–37, 226
period panties, 76–77, 80
Perl, 12
personal advisory board (PAB), 60–62, 129, 182
personal computers, 68–69
pets, 62
Phoenix Fund, 187
photographers, volume of shots taken by, 31–32
PitchBook, 119, 221
pitch decks
    about, 51
    in data room, 210
    for digitalundivided, 93
    examples of, 93n
    Kawasaki's 10/20/30 rule for, 219
    and small business/startups comparison, 7
    for venture capital, 210, 218–19
pivoting
    and building the MVP, 98
    willingness to, 37–38, 226
potential, 33–35, 226
premium (defined), 69n
preparation, 18, 33
Price, Lisa, *43*
Primary, *46*
private equity, 167. *See also* funding
problem solved by your business, 73–74. *See also* ideas
process, 35–36, 226
product-market fit, 83–121
    and Business Model Canvas (BMC), 111–17
    and digitalundivided, 92, 121
    and funding decisions, 170, 175–76
    and Squire's success story, 85–87
    of startups vs. small businesses, 8
    and team fit, 123
    See also Build-Measure-Learn (B-M-L) loop; Minimal Viable Products (MVP)
products, physical, *89*
profit margin, 69n
ProjectDiane, 118–21, 193–94
project management software, 156
public transportation, 74

registering your companies, 154
repeat customers, 72, 75–76
retirement savings, 15, 15n, 180
revenue stream, 114
reverse auction business model, *115*
#ReWriteTheCode documentary, 194
Rise of the Rest, 38
risk
    and co-founders, 132
    and core values, *138*
    and entrepreneurial mindset, 18
    as part of the journey, 25
    as privilege of Entitleds, 25
    reducing, through preparation, 33
Ruby Love, *43*
"rules" founders are told to follow, 44–45

SAFEs (simple agreement for future equity), 206–7
savings, funding the company with your, 168–69, *178*
scale/scaling of startups
    and funding options, 169, 170, 206, 212, 217
    importance of team in, 164
    and small businesses compared to startups, 7, *7*
scarcity mindset, 141–42
Schlitz brewery, 22
self-assessments, conducting, 57–60
self-awareness, commitment to, *140*
self-care, importance of, 17–18, 19, 124–25
Seneca, 33n
severance packages, 163, 163n
sexual harassment in startup world, 118
Silicon Valley
    minorities represented in, 90–91
    myths about, 38
    and New York startup community, xvi
    startups outside of, 38
skills gaps, 131
small businesses compared to startups, 6–9, *7*
social groups (offline), *104*
social knowledge, 34–35
social media platforms, *104*, 190
software, MVPs for, *89*
speed of build with startups, *7*, 8
spiritual health, spending time on, 19
Spotify, 38
Squarespace, 14, 88n, 95, 95n
Squire's success story, 85–87

INDEX

stacks, xviii (note), xviii, 211
stakeholders, prioritizing the experience of, 36–37
standards, high, 36–37
Star Trek, 28–30
startups and startup industry
  about startups, 5–9
  biases in, xx, 13
  capital for (*see* funding)
  as closed system, xvii
  lack of diversity in, 118–20, 194, 194*n*
  lies about limited options for, 45–47
  as means to achieving goals, 4
  meritocratic/accepting veneer of, xvii
  outside of Silicon Valley, 38
  pattern matching practiced in, xvi–xvii, xx
  small businesses compared to, 6–9, *7*
  why you should build your, 9–13
stereotypes
  challenges associated with, 225
  "covering" to downplay negative, xix (*note*)
stock options, 145
Strategist archetype, 150–51
strengths, identifying, 57–60, 226
subscription business model, *114*
success, internal process of, 18–19
support network, failing to get buy-in from, 129–30
SWOT analysis, 57–60, 61, 226

taxes, paying, 152
  teams, 123–64
  accountants on, 154
  and buy-in from support system, 129–30
  and company values, 136–43
  consultants, 135, 145, 146–47
  and daily check-ins, 159–60
  and delegation, 149
  and difficult conversations, 160
  Doer archetype, 148–49
  Economist archetype, 151–52
  executive coaches on, 154–55
  founders and co-founders, 130–35
  friends/family members on, 127–29
  lawyers on, 153
  and leadership skills, 124–26
  Lieutenant archetype, 149–50
  market fit and team fit, 123
  and Objectives and Key Results framework, 157–59, 159*n*

outlining responsibilities in, 133–34
recruiting, 36
and staying agile, 156–57
Strategist archetype, 150–51
when to bring in outside help, 135
See also employees
tech bros, xvi–xvii, xxi, 13, 41. *See also* Entitleds
TechCrunch, 194, 221
technology
  benefits of, to entrepreneurs, 9, 13–14
  and building *The Budget Fashionista*, 9, *11*, 12
  and small businesses compared to startups, 7–8, *7*
  and stacks, xviii (*note*), xviii, 211
term sheets, 220–21
Terry's Taco Truck (example)
  elevator pitch for, 79–80
  funding options for, 170
  Minimal Viable Products for, 94–96, *95*
  problem statement for, 78–79
  and researching industry culture, 151
  soliciting honest feedback on, 102
threats, identifying, 58, 60
toolbox for personal success, 51–64
  conducting self-assessments, 57–60
  creating a Personal Advisory Board, 60–62
  finding your exit number, 63–64
  knowing yourself, 56–57
  mindfulness practices, 52–53
  recognizing your core values, 53–56
  See also mindset
trust
  as core value, *137, 139*
  in employees/team members, *137*, 142, 149, 159
  and honesty, *139*
truth, speaking, *139*
Tumblr, xvi (*note*), xvi
Twitter
  and educational background of founder, *43*
  as pivot from failed platform, 37
  researching problems/pain points on, 73
  and venture capitalists, 190

Ugly Baby Test, 100–101, 102
Ulmer, Mikaila, 99
Uncommonly, 155

INDEX

United Kingdom, government finance programs in, 185, 185*n*
Upwork, 119
U.S. Small Business Administration (SBA), 6

value proposition, 112
venture capital/capitalists, 204–21
   asking for money too soon, 192–93
   attracting, 190
   and *The Budget Fashionista*, 167–68
   considering losing control vs. potential gains, 212
   convertible notes, 207
   and core values, 221
   and data room/doc room, 209–11
   definition of, 2*n*
   and definition of startups, 6
   elevator pitch for, 218
   and ethnic minority startups, 119, 168
   funding rounds, 216–17
   general partners (GPs), 119*n*, 204–5
   high costs of some options, 212
   how to pitch, 218
   limited partners (LPs), 204, 205
   math behind, 205–6
   and Nasty Gal's bankruptcy, 213–16
   and owner's equity, 209, 210*n*
   proactively seeking out, 190–92
   pros/cons of, 168, *180*
   questions for assessing your VC, 208–9
   and SAFEs (simple agreement for future equity), 206–7
   and term sheets, 220–21
   and women founders, 216*n*
Venture Deals (Feld and Mendelson), 207*n*
vesting options, 145
vulnerability, 31, 142–43

Warby Parker, 45, *46*
weaknesses, identifying, 57–60, 226
wealth creation, 9, 75
website builders, 88, 88*n*, 95
WeTransfer, 38
white guys from elite schools, 41–42. *See also* tech bros
Williams, Serena, 52
Winfrey, Oprah, 27
Wix, 88*n*, 95*n*
Wonderschool, *46*
WordPress, 12*n*, *43*, 88*n*

Xerox, 68

Y Combinator, xvii
YouTube, 37, *43*

Zapier, 39*n*
Zappos, 99
Zoom, 160

Penguin Random House LLC
1745 Broadway
US-NY, 10019
US
https://www.penguinrandomhouse.com
1-800-733-3000

The authorized representative in the EU for product safety and compliance is

Penguin Random House Ireland
Morrison Chambers, 32 Nassau Street
D02 YH68
IE
https://eu-contact.penguin.ie

ISBN: 9798217182442
Release ID: 154026569

www.ingramcontent.com/pod-product-compliance
Lightning Source LLC
Chambersburg PA
CBHW030852170426
43193CB00009BA/579